William McKee

History of Sherbro Mission, West Africa

Under the Direction of the Missionary Society

William McKee

History of Sherbro Mission, West Africa
Under the Direction of the Missionary Society

ISBN/EAN: 9783337125660

Printed in Europe, USA, Canada, Australia, Japan

Cover: Foto ©ninafisch / pixelio.de

More available books at **www.hansebooks.com**

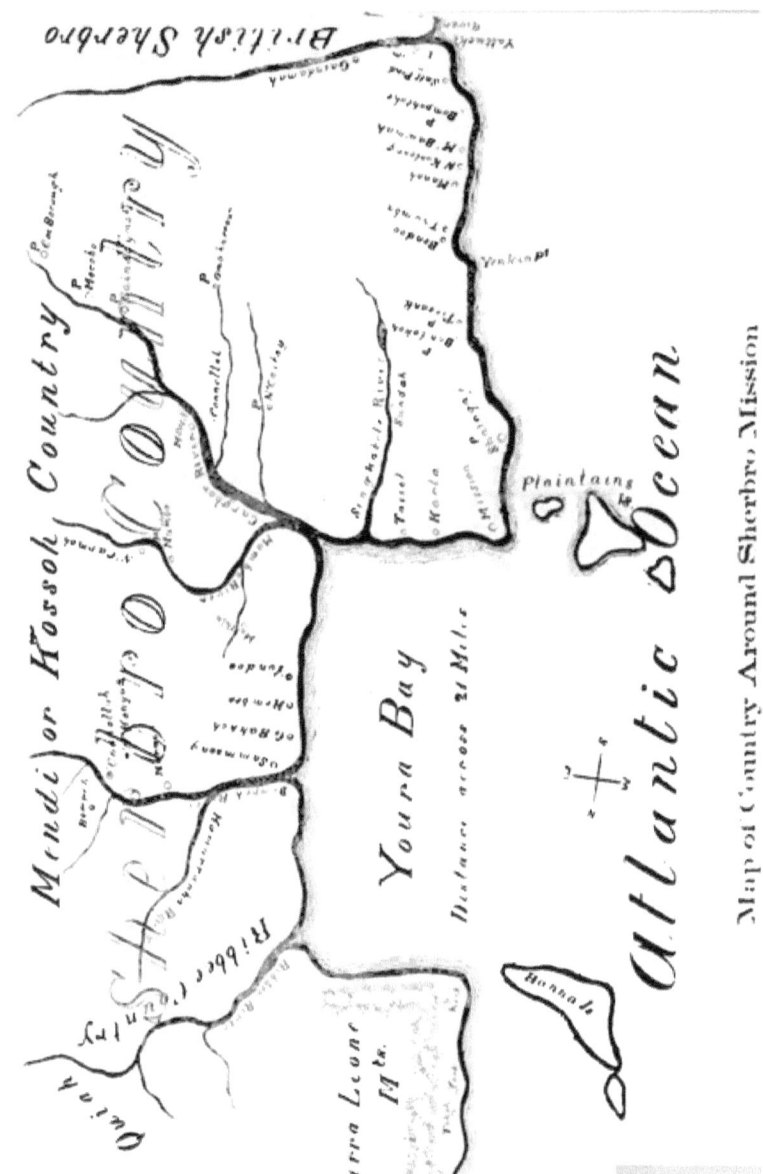

Map of Country Around Sherbro Mission.

HISTORY

— OF —

SHERBRO MISSION.

WEST AFRICA,

UNDER THE

DIRECTION OF THE MISSIONARY SOCIETY

OF THE

United Brethren in Christ.

———

DAYTON, OHIO:
UNITED BRETHREN PUBLISHING HOUSE,
1874.

CONTENTS.

CHAPTER I.
Origin of the Mission.. 9

CHAPTER II.
Freetown—First impressions—Kindness of American Missionary Association—Exploring Tours—Return of Messrs. Shuey and Kumler.................................. 14

CHAPTER III.
Mr. Flickinger left alone—Kindness of other Missionaries—Head-men's Maneuvering—Purchase of a House in Freetown.. 22

CHAPTER IV.
Two more Missionaries Appointed—Efforts to Locate at Shengay Successful—Chief Caulker's Design—Location Described.. 27

CHAPTER V.
Learning the Sherbro Language—Rev. W. B. Witt—Building Mission Chapel—Sabbath-school organized—Building Mission Residence—Failure of Mr. Bilheimer's Health.. 34

CHAPTER VI.
Rev. John A. Williams—His Life and Death—Bible-class and Sabbath-school—Two Souls Converted—Their Firmness in the Truth—Crowds Flock to Hear.......... 40

CHAPTER VII.
Rev. C. O. Wilson—Discouragements—His Return............ 44

CONTENTS.

CHAPTER VIII.

Mr. Flickinger's Third Voyage to Africa—Sale of Freetown property—Apathy of the Church—Slave-holders Rebellion in America.. 48

CHAPTER IX.

Mr. Bilheimer's Visit to America—Marriage—Returns to Africa—Joy of the People—Proof of God's Approval... 54

CHAPTER X.

Climate—Seasons—Sickness 59

CHAPTER XI.

Religion—Superstition—The Gospel their only hope...... 65

CHAPTER XII.

Agriculture—Horticulture 70

CHAPTER XIII.

Sickness of Missionaries—Mr. Bilheimer's final return to America—Mr. Williams Alone—Prospects............ 74

CHAPTER XIV.

Mr. and Mrs. Hadley—Arrival in Africa—Difficulty of Reaching the Heathen——Meeting of the Board......... 82

CHAPTER XV.

First Year—Strong Faith—Discouragements—Mohammedans 88

CHAPTER XVI.

Day and Sabbath-schools—War—Mr. and Mrs. Hadley return to America—His Death....................................... 95

CHAPTER XVII.

Effect of Mr. Hadley's Death—Doubts and Diffidence of the Board—General Conference Action...................... 101

CHAPTER XVIII.

Appointment of Mr. and Mrs. Gomer—Meeting in Dayton—Arrival in Shengay... 109

CHAPTER XIX.

Difficulty of Holding Converts—Children under the influence of Heathen Parents 118

CHAPTER XX.

Mr. Gomer's Faithfulness—Visits Harrowtown—Day and Sabbath-schools—Interest of the King in the Mission...... 126

CHAPTER XXI.

Conversion of King Caulker...... 132

CHAPTER XXII.

Other Souls Converted—Cheering Prospect—More Help Wanted...... 138

CHAPTER XXIII.

Death of the King—The Field Large and Ripe...... 144

CHAPTER XXIV.

Farming—Commerce—Wages—Courtship—Marriage...... 150

CHAPTER XXV.

The New King—Catalogue of Converts...... 158

CHAPTER XXVI.

Two more Missionaries Sent—Letters from Mrs. Hadley, and Mr. Gomer...... 165

CHAPTER XXVII.

D. F. Wilberforce...... 178

CHAPTER XXVIII.

Interesting Letters—War Palaver—Mr. Gomer as a Diplomat...... 183

CHAPTER XXIX.

Building a New Chapel—Rev. Peter Warner and Wife go to Africa...... 195

CHAPTER XXX.

Sherbro Country and People—Kings' Quarrels—Number of Converts...... 202

CONTENTS.

CHAPTER XXXI.
Closing Remarks.. 220

MISSION IN GERMANY.

CHAPTER I.
Origin of the Mission.. 225

CHAPTER II.
Opposition of certain classes....................................... 231

HOME MISSIONS.

CHAPTER I.
Origin of the Missionary Society................................. 238

CHAPTER II.
Mission-conferences—Statistics.................................. 250

CHAPTER III.
Organization of Nebraska Conference—General Satistics... 259

CHAPTER IV.
Fourteenth General Conference—Wisconsin made a Mission-conference again—Cascade Conference organized... 264

CHAPTER V.
Twelve Mission - conferences—North Michigan Self-supporting—German Missions in Toledo, and Columbus... 268

CHAPTER VI.
Increase in Numbers—Improvement in Book-keeping—Financial Exhibit of Twenty Years—The Sixteenth General Conference in Dayton, Ohio........................ 273

PREFACE.

The following pages have been prepared with a view to presenting in brief the history of Sherbro Mission, in West Africa, under the auspices of the Church of the United Brethren in Christ. Fully persuaded that this mission has the seal of the Master's approbation, and has been kept alive and carried through many seasons of darkness and great discouragement by His gracious providence, the writer trusts that this record of its career may prove both interesting and profitable to the souls of its readers, and a stimulus to bring the Church up to a more hearty and liberal support of this and all other missions under the fostering care of the Board of Missions.

Added to the volume will be found an interesting account of the origin of the United Brethren Mission in the kingdom of Bavaria. The reader will see from this description what painstaking and labor are required, and what difficulties are encountered in establishing a foreign mission, even in countries where the least opposition might be expected.

The volume closes with a summary of the Home Mission work of the United Brethren Church for the last twenty years.

It gives an account of the formation of the Missionary Society, the causes which led to such organization, and the more immediate and important results to the Church, and to the world, of the operations of said society within the limits of the United States.

The writer commits this little volume to the world with the prayer that God's blessing may attend it, and that His grace, in the largest measure, may still abide with all who are engaged in missionary labor in heathen lands.

WM. McKEE.

DAYTON, OHIO, March 1, 1874.

SHERBRO MISSION.

CHAPTER I.

Origin of the Mission.

IT has ever been the hope of Christians that the whole world will be subdued by the gospel. They have always held that the prophecies relating to Jesus Christ warrant the belief that he will at some period become the Lord of the whole earth, in the sense of causing the whole world to trust in him as the only savior from sin. This conviction has so moved the hearts of God's people during the last half century, that they have projected missions for the conversion of the heathen in Arabia, Syria, Turkey, India, China, Japan, Australia, Madagascar, Greenland, Africa, North America, South America, and in scores of the islands of the Pacific Ocean.

Among the efforts recently put forth may be mentioned the first foreign mission undertaken by the Church of the United Brethren in Christ, among the Sherbro tribe, on the western coast of Africa. The station was located at the town of Shengay, in the fifth degree of north latitude, and thirteenth degree of west longitude, from Greenwich.

The subject of sending missionaries to foreign countries had engaged the attention of many members of the Church, both ministers and laymen, for several years. The Rev. W. J. Shuey was especially prompt and energetic in agitating the mind of the Church on this subject. He pleaded for it before the Miami Conference, of which he is a member, and visited several other conferences, dwelling upon the degraded, perishing condition of those who were destitute of the gospel, and maintaining with great earnestness that this Church could not do its whole duty while it made no effort to send the gospel to the heathen. These appeals had a good effect. The leading members of the Church began to think and pray. They felt burdened with the fact that God had done so much for them and they were doing so little in turn for his cause. They believed, too, on reflection, that the heathen were our neighbors and brethren, and that we were in an important sense "our brother's keeper." This being so, they ought to perform their part in enlightening them. This, however, was a conviction which was of slow growth with many. There were not wanting members of the Church who thought a foreign mission a useless project. They found many and weighty objections. There was work enough to do at home; it was not God's time to save the heathen; as a Church we were not numerous or wealthy enough for such an undertaking, and we would, on the whole, be wasting our energies attempting what we could not accomplish and at the same time be neglecting what we might do in home fields which were ripe for the sickle. However, after considerable discussion in divers places and manners, earnest thought, and fervent prayer, the leading minds in the Church were led to the conclusion that it was our solemn duty to help carry the gospel to the heathen as well as to the civilized nations. And when it was asked, Where shall we go? all seemed to agree that we should go to the most needy.

India, China, and other heathen countries were spoken of; but it was finally agreed that Africa was as far from God as any portion of the earth's inhabitants, and it would be well for us to make an effort to help them. It was thought especially fitting that this country, which had kidnapped so many Africans, brought them to this country and made slaves of them, should now do something to enlighten and save the millions who in their own native country grope their way in darkness down to death. However, before this conviction became general in the Church, or had given expression to itself in any more positive manner than the making of frequent contributions to other boards of missions sustaining laborers in foreign lands, the Missionary Board of the United Brethren Church held its first annual meeting in Westerville, Ohio, June 1, 1854. It is worthy of note that this Board at its first session was burdened with the duty of sending missionaries to foreign countries. After much thought and prayer they gave expression to their feelings in the following words:

"*Resolved*, That we send one or more missionaries to Africa as soon as practicable."

Memorable words! A dozen men representing a comparatively feeble church resolving to send the gospel to Africa! Surely this was not the counsel of worldly wisdom! The Board walked by faith, not by sight. And the history of their mission in Africa demonstrates the assertion that they received wisdom from above.

The Board then appointed the Rev. W. J. Shuey, pastor of the First United Brethren Church in Cincinnati, as their first missionary to Africa, and recommended the Executive Committee to appoint one or two more to accompany him. Not long after, the committee chose Rev. D. C. Kumler and Rev. D. K. Flickinger to go to Africa with Mr. Shuey.

Bidding farewell to friends and country, they sailed from New York early in January, 1855, and in due time arrived at Sierre Leone West Africa.

CHAPTER II.

Freetown—First Impressions—Kindness of American Missionary Association—Exploring Tours—Return of Messrs. Shuey and Kumler.

OUR missionaries landed in Freetown, February 26, 1855, having been thirty-four days on the ocean. As they were wholly unaccustomed to sea voyages the reader may imagine their satisfaction on being able to again set foot on *terra firma*. Freetown is a city of eighteen or twenty thousand inhabitants with not more than two or three hundred white people in it. It is the capital city of the colony of Sierre Leone—so named from a great mountain in the colony denominated Sierre Leone, or "Lion Mountain." The colony, or state, contains nearly three hundred square miles, being about as large as a small county in this country.

The city is unlike anything in America. The people know nothing about the use of horses, wagons, carraiges, or drays. Traveling by land is all done on foot. Goods, building materials, and agricultural products are carried from one place to another by the natives; and as a rule whatever they can place on their heads they walk off with, and with as steady and upright a gait as if this was the original design in giving the people heads.

Many of the people live in huts made of poles, thatched with straw or wild grass, and then plastered or *daubed* with mud both within and without.

But there are some excellent houses. The town is regularly laid off, and some of the streets are well graded and paved. This colony is owned and governed by England. Queen Victoria appoints the governor.

Here our brethren tarried a few days, feeling that they were strangers in a strange land. But everything they saw and heard reminded them that this was a heathen country. The people needed somebody to tell them that Jesus died for them, loved them, and would save them if they believed in him. They had heard and thought much about the poor heathen before they left home; now they saw them. They felt, moreover, that they had done well to have it in their hearts to carry the gospel to them. There were several good churches in Freetown. These were fruits of missionary labor, and our missionaries were strengthened in the conviction that the gospel is the power of God unto salvation for all people, of whatever race or color. Here they might have tarried and found plenty of work to do, but they were unwilling to build on another man's foundation. Hence they determined to go out into some darker place and hold forth the lamp of life. The field was very large. It would not do for all the laborers, however pleasant to themselves, to congregate in Freetown.

They now sailed down the coast a distance of one hundred and twenty miles, to the south part of Sherbro Island, and took lodgings at Good Hope Station, a mission planted and manned by the American Missionary Association. To this association and their missionaries in Africa our missionaries and our missionary society, from first to last, are under many obligations. They have shown us numerous and marked favors. They gave our first missionaries letters of introduction and commendation to their own missionaries in

Africa. To the Rev. Geo. Thompson and others in charge of Mendi Mission in Africa, Mr. Whipple, the corresponding secretary of the association, wrote, among other good and kind and cheering words:

"In relation to all the questions of church polity we understand them to be so catholic in spirit that they can cordially labor, and without any disposition to proselyte, in connection with evangelical churches of every denomination which are not themselves exclusive in creed or practice. We trust also that the love of Christ so far constrains them that they will be ready to know nothing among you but Christ and him crucified as the groundwork of our hope, and the Redeemer through whom we may be accepted of God."

I need scarcely add that our brethren were kindly received and bidden God speed by all the employes of the American Missionary Association. Denominational lines were forgotten or kept in the background, and the question coming up from all hearts was "What can we do to bring the people to Christ; how shall we reach and save the multitudes who are perishing in their sins?"

From Good Hope they visited many points of interest. It was their desire to secure some location which they might call their own, and go to work as early as possible to erect suitable buildings and commence the work of a regular mission-station. But they soon learned that this was not the work of a day. Being strangers to the country, the people, the climate, the customs of the people, and the centers of influence,—for even heathen people have such centers,—they soon discovered that it would be an easy matter to adopt the penny wise and pound foolish policy. They might select some site and spend time and money on it only to discover by and by that it would not do at all. They had neither time nor money to waste. So they made a number of explorations up the rivers, as well as up and down the coast; made inquiries of other missionaries and of natives. All the places visited were so objectionable as to cause them to hesitate to pitch their tent. They spent some time at Mendi Mission, under the control of that great and good man, Rev. George Thompson. Mr. Kumler, in company with Mr. Brooks, made a voyage up the Big Boom River. He saw many objects of interest, and especially much need of evangelistic labor; but the dangers growing out of the climate, the swamps, the wild animals, and the wild natives, were so many and serious that he could fix upon no spot where he deemed it the part of wisdom to establish a mission.

At length Mr. Shuey and Mr. Flickinger sailed up the Jong River to explore the interior somewhat, and if possible secure a location for a mission. Passing Weela, and other towns of interest, they reached at length a kind of horseshoe bend in the river, about sixty miles from the coast, on which was situated a town named MoKelli with a population of five or six hundred. Adding to this other villages on the bend of the river, there was in quite a small compass a population of nearly two thousand souls. Here our missionaries determined to commence work as soon as possible. The country was excellent. The people were hungry for the bread of life. The climate and healthfulness of the place were as good as any they could hope to find in the interior of the country. But before they could even commence the work they must obtain a title from the head-man of the tribe, or king of the country. They sought an interview with him and obtained the promise of a written title to mission grounds, but before the bargain was concluded—which with these people is generally a tedious process—they returned to Freetown. Mr. Shuey having now accomplished, as he supposed, the main object of his voyage to Africa,—the location of the mission,—and Mr. Kumler being dangerously ill with African fever, it was deemed advisable that they should both return to America. Accordingly they took ship and sailed for New York, which port they reached in safety after a voyage of forty-two days, and arrived at home soon after. Mr. Kumler was a long time recovering from his illness, the African fever tenaciously clinging to him for several months after his return. In a few months the Board of Missions held its annual meeting in Cincinnati. Of course, Mr. Shuey and Mr. Kumler both attended the meeting in order to communicate the results of their travels, labors, and observations. The Rev. John Bright, who was then the corresponding secretary of the Missionary Society, was inclined to reflect somewhat on our brethren for their early return. Among other things, he inadvertently let fall the remark that if some of our missionaries would remain in Africa even though they *died* there it would have a good effect on the Church.

Mr. Kumler said in reply that he felt very much like he would die *here* before long, and if it were deemed advisable *they might take his bones to Africa and bury them there!* Mr. Bright made no further complaint.

CHAPTER III.

Mr. Flickinger Left Alone—Kindness of Other Missionaries—Head-men's Maneuvering—Purchase of a House in Freetown.

MR. FLICKINGER was now the only one left in Africa to represent the United Brethren Church. He proceeded to Good Hope Station, on Sherbro Island, where he spent considerable of his time for nearly a year. He served, in fact, as the pastor of the congregation a good part of the time. In July, 1855, he was attacked with fever, and although he partially recovered, he never fully regained his former state of health. Still, he would not consent to abandon the field. He would sally forth from Good Hope Station, or from Freetown, and make quite extensive tours of observation, preaching to the people meantime, until his strength was exhausted, and then return to his post. He found the missionaries of the American Missionary Association fast friends during his stay. All the missionaries he met, in fact, whether from England or America, treated him with the utmost kindness. But those of the American Missionary Association, a half dozen of whom went over in the same vessel in which he sailed, were especially helpful to him in his labors among the Africans. Of course, the subject that most engaged his attention was the securing of a suitable location for a station. He found it difficult to close a bargain with any of the heathen kings. They would talk, and sometimes promise, but when it came to giving a written title they were slow, and very uncertain. The king of MoKelli, when Mr. Shuey and himself had decided to commence operations, never committed himself to paper. He hesitated, talked, or "palavered," as the Africans would say, half promised, but never made the deed. Meantime Mr. Flickinger began to learn from the other missionaries, and from observation, that MoKelli was too remote from the coast for a mission-station. A part of the year the Jong River was not navigable as far as MoKelli, and it was a laborious, dangerous, and costly voyage, which it would by no means justify our missionaries to make so often, as they would be obliged to do if our mission were located there.

During the summer the chief, or head-man of the town of Shengay, was driven from his home by a war with the neighboring tribes, and took refuge in the town of Bendoo, only four miles from Good Hope Station. Mr. Flickinger paid him a visit and tried hard to obtain permission to open a mission in or near his town, which was located on the mainland sixty miles south-east of Freetown, and about the same distance north-west of Good Hope Station, on Sherbro Island. Mr. Thomas Stephen Caulker, the head-man, was not inclined to grant any such privilege. Believing it to be the best site he had seen, Mr. F. visited the old man again and again, and offered every inducement he could bring to bear on the mind of Mr. Caulker to induce him to grant the request. But in vain. The old man could neither be coaxed, nor hired to yield; and for the present Mr. F. had to abandon the hope of locating at Shengay.

Time passed. Mr. F. visited various places on the coast, and made two long journeys inland, one on the Big Boom River, traveling more than a hundred miles in a frail canoe rowed by the natives. During these travels he declares he saw some of the finest country he ever looked on in his life. But no site for a mission was obtained. It was too soon to begin so far from the coast.

He continued thus to labor and prospect till in December, when he was again prostrated with fever. From this attack he did not recover sufficiently to do any very effective service as a missionary. Accordingly he remained most of the time in Freetown, hoping to so far regain his health as to resume his labors. But he was doomed to disappointment. He grew worse instead of better; and in April, 1856, he was compelled to return to America. Before leaving Freetown, however, he purchased a house for the benefit of the missionaries who might follow him. Whether our mission-station were located at MoKelli, Shengay, or some other point, it would certainly be in the neighborhood of Freetown; and the missionaries would often need to resort to Freetown for rest and medical assistance. For this property he paid five hundred pounds sterling—twenty-four hundred dollars. The Board of

Missions had been consulted, and heartily concurred in the idea of making this house in Freetown a base of supplies and missionary hospital for future operations. It was hoped that a select school might be also opened here for the instruction of advanced scholars, particularly those who might make effective teachers and pastors. The only reason why this house did not meet the expectations of the Board is that the mission in Africa was never properly manned, that is, as to the number of missionaries employed. There was never, until a recent period, more than one or two engaged at one time.

From April, 1856, to January, 1857, a period of nine months, we had no missionary in Africa. But the work had not been abandoned. The Church was learning its first lessons in foreign mission-work. And, if it was a little slow, it was determined and persevering. It had put its hand to the plow and did not dare to look back. So it waited, and prayed, and hoped. Believing it had a work to do in Africa, it trusted in God; and when it could not go forward it stood still until the pillar of fire moved forward. Then the Church was ready to follow after.

CHAPTER IV.

Two More Missionaries Appointed—Efforts to Locate at Shengay Successful—Chief Caulker's Design—Location Described.

THE Church did not wait long. A number of names were presented to the Executive Committee for appointment to the mission in Africa. From these names the committee selected and appointed Dr. W. B. Witt, of Cincinnati, and the Rev. J. K. Billheimer, of Virginia. Mr. Witt was an excellent physician and a faithful minister of the gospel. Mr. Billheimer was a young man of more than ordinary piety and fully consecrated to the work of saving souls. These appointments of the committee were hailed by the church at large as being quite happy in themselves, and an earnest of the successful prosecution of the foreign mission.

All things being ready, the missionaries named, accompanied by Mr. Flickinger, who was still retained as the superintendent of the Sherbro Mission, took ship at New York and sailed for Africa, arriving at Freetown early in January, 1857. In a short time they made their way to Good Hope and other stations of the Mendi Mission. This mission, under the management of the American Missionary Association, is so called because that portion of Africa which they occupy is called the Mendi country. At these several stations our brethren found welcome homes and plenty to do whenever they were able to work.

Mr. Flickinger again renewed his efforts to secure a location at Shengay. Chief Caulker was still at Bendoo, being afraid to return to his native town lest the neighboring head-men would kill him. He now listened to our missionaries' proposals with some interest. Still, he was not ready to grant the request. Pending these negotiations, or "palavers," with the chief, Mr. F. made a voyage to Liberia, a flourishing republic about two hundred miles down the coast, in a south-easterly direction from Sierre Leone. He spent nearly a month here, and gave it as his opinion that the president, congress, and other public functionaries, together with a number of the missionaries whom he met, ought to be taught some lessons on industry and self-denial. He feared they were not doing their whole duty to civilize and Christianize the republic. He was also fully persuaded that Sierre Leone was a more healthy country than Liberia, and returned to Good Hope determined to renew his efforts to obtain a foot-hold at Shengay. Mr. Caulker was now more yielding, and after several "palavers" with him, he was induced to give his consent to the location of our mission at Shengay, in the month of March, 1857.

>"God moves in a mysterious way
>His wonders to perform."

This beautiful song was never more plainly illustrated than in the present case. This old chief, reeking with crimes numerous and fiendish, granting permission for the planting of a mission on his territory, shows how God sometimes causes the wrath of man to praise him. As has been already said, he was driven from home by neighboring warriors and dared not return. Now, he doubtless thought that a mission-station located near Shengay, and the constant occupancy of the place by white men, and possibly the occasional passing of a British man-of-war, and other vessels, would render him secure from his enemies. He cared not for the gospel himself. He did not wish his people to become Christianized. All he wanted was protection from his heathen enemies. He believed he could secure this protection by means of a mission-station; and, then, as for Christianizing the people, he could easily prevent that. He would give just as little countenance as possible to the labors of the missionaries. The free people he could advise not to attend the school or the church, and his slaves he could prohibit, once for all, from going near the mission. "Man proposes; God disposes." Mr. Caulker sought his own safety in the establishment of Shengay Mission, but God intended to glorify himself in the salvation of the people.

Soon after the work of clearing the ground and building the mission chapel begun the old head-man returned to Shengay and again took up his abode. Not long after this he made peace with all the tribes about him, so that he was in no further dread of being killed.

Now he would have been glad if the mission had not been commenced. But there it was. He had given a written title to our missionaries for the land. He could not buy it back, or induce them to give it up. But he determined the mission should do nothing to save the people if he could help it. The missionaries might, indeed, educate his own children, but they should not make Christians of them. And this policy of hedging up the way of the missionaries by his influence as a king he pursued with considerable success for a number of years. He would neither enter the kingdom himself nor suffer others that would have entered to go in. But as I shall have frequent occasion to refer to Chief Caulker in this history, I dismiss him for the present.

Mr. Flickinger now returned to America, having been elected by the General Conference to the office of corresponding secretary of the missionary society. As the rainy season was just commencing, Messrs. Witt and Billheimer thought it not prudent to commence the work of erecting buildings till the next dry season. Meantime they continued to make their homes at the stations of the Mendi Mission, and to teach and preach as the Lord gave them opportunity and health to labor.

Before closing this chapter I will treat my readers to a description of Shengay Mission-station from the pen of one of our missionaries:

"It is on the mainland, about sixty-five miles from Freetown, in an east by south direction. It is a cape, twenty or thirty feet above high-tide, and bounded on three sides by salt-water. To the north and east is the Yawry bay; to the west and south is the wide, wide sea. A few rods from the north point is Williams Island; and in a line with it, some four miles at sea, we have three fine islands, called Plantain Islands.

"The land is rich and arable, and is covered with some very fine teak, or African oak, and a large number of majestic palms. It can be easily cleared, and will cost less to prepare for our use than the land of any other place of which we have any knowledge. The water is pure; and that is an important consideration in this country, where pure water is rare. There is a fine sandy beach extending around this place; and there is rock enough for building purposes. About one half mile from this point is the town which gives name to this cape, and all the surrounding country. It occupies no more ground than a single square in the city of Dayton, and contains about three hundred inhabitants. Their houses are made of a few posts put into the ground, and small sticks of the mangrove woven in between them. They are covered with mud. They are about ten feet high, roofed with grass, and so near together that there are only small paths left between them. These paths are so crooked, that persons passing through them easily become bewildered. They are generally made in a circular form, though some are made square, oblong, and otherwise. The people's council-house stands next to the sea, and differs from the rest by being much larger. Its walls are only three or three and a half feet high, and the ceiling is open to the grass roof above. It has two doorways; and all around on the inside, next to the wall, there is a platform raised one or one and a half feet, and about three feet wide, over which hang, suspended from the roof, *hammocks for lounging in!* It is plastered with white mud that resembles lime, and is the neatest house of the kind I have seen in Africa."

CHAPTER V.

Learning the Sherbro Language—Rev. W. B. Witt—Building Mission Chapel—Sabbath-school Organized—Building Mission Residence—Failure of Mr. Billheimer's Health.

ONE of the chief obstacles in the way of bringing the heathen to the knowledge of salvation is the difficulty of understanding them, or they us. They speak in one language, we another. It is true many of the Africans speak a dialect as near English as anything else, but it is such a gibberish that it takes a stranger a good while to learn it, and even then he finds it so meager, that he can not convey to them any correct ideas of the holiness of God, the redemption of the world through Jesus Christ, and kindred subjects, all important for them to understand. In order to overcome this difficulty, Mr. Witt undertook the task of learning the Sherbro language, which is spoken by a great many Africans. But as they have no written language, this was a tedious process. He had not gone through the first rainy season, however, until his health commenced to fail so rapidly that he began to fear he would be obliged soon to return to America. The missionary Board, hearing of the precarious state of his health, passed a resolution at Lebanon, Pa., May, 1858, expressing their willingness to have him return if the state of his health was such as to prevent his further usefulness in Africa. Accordingly Mr. Witt returned, after an absence of one year and a half. He rendered valuable service to the mission while there, and was ever after a zealous advocate and supporter of the Sherbro Mission.

When the great Rebellion broke out in the United States, Mr. Witt was among the number who offered themselves on the altar of their country. He was the surgeon of a regiment of soldiers from the State of Indiana. After passing through a number of hard-fought battles, including that of Millikin's Bend, one of the most terrible conflicts of the war, and undergoing many hardships, he was one day crossing a narrow bay in the Gulf of Mexico, on the coast of Texas, when the pontoon bridge gave way, and Mr. Witt, in company with scores of other brave soldiers, found a watery grave.

To return from this digression, Mr. Billhiemer employed some of the natives, as soon as the rainy season in the spring of 1857 began to wear away, and proceeded to clear and otherwise improve the mission grounds. The first thing of importance to be done was the building of a chapel. On consultation with the Board and with the Mendi missionaries it was believed that the cheapest and speediest method of building a chapel was to have one made ready to set up in New York and ship it to Africa. The Executive Committee therefore ordered a building twenty-four by thirty feet square. The house arrived at Shengay in good time and in good order; and in the month of June, 1857, Mr. Bilhiemer had the satisfaction of seeing the chapel completed and ready for occupancy. He had it set on stone pillars seven feet high. This was a necessary precaution to avoid the dampness so common and so productive of disease on all the western coast of Africa. While the work was going on—a slow process truly with none but the careless, lazy, stupid work-hands that he was obliged to em-

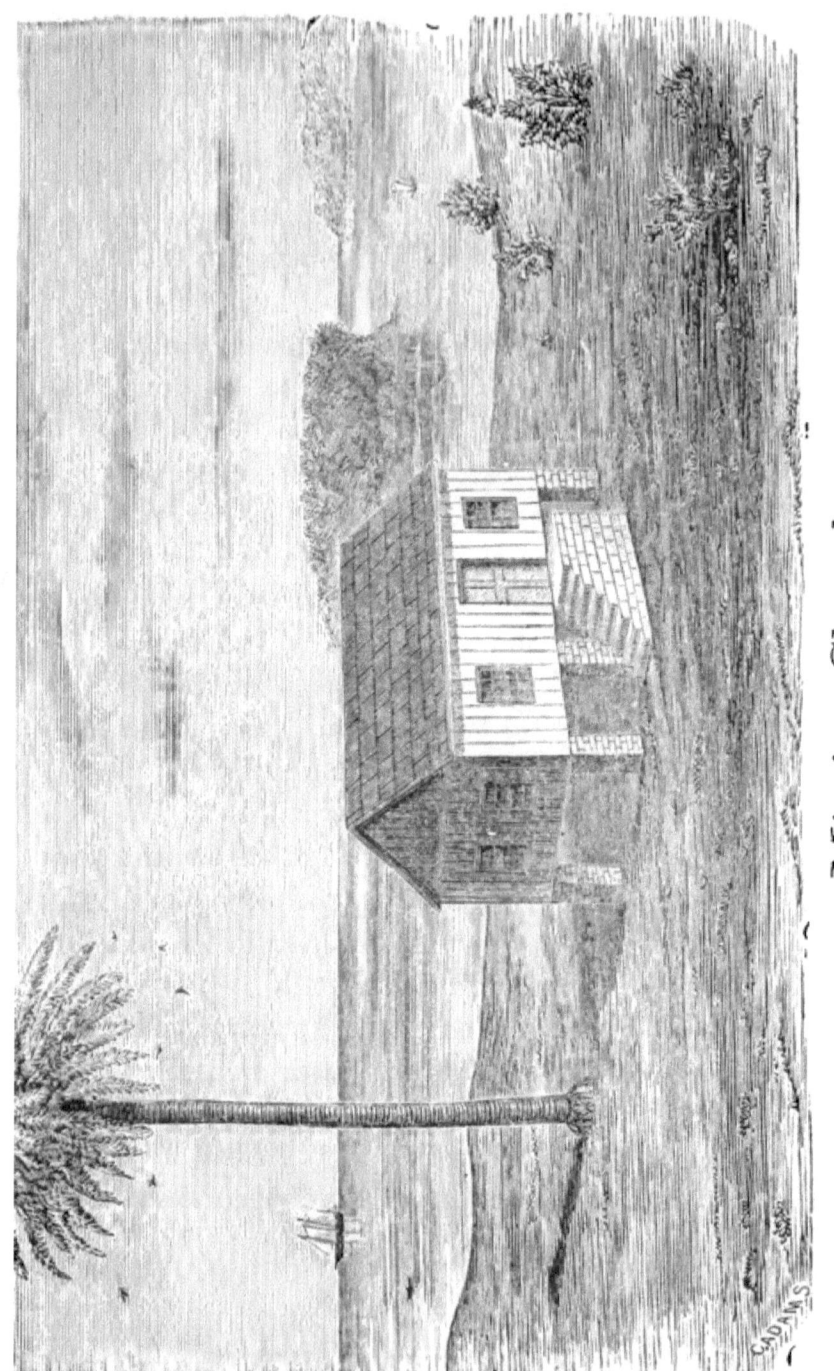

Mission Chapel.

ploy—Mr. B. lived in a native hut, superintending every part of the work himself. He put a partition through the new house and made a bed-room and store-room for himself, leaving a room twenty by twenty-four feet square for a school-house and church.

Thankful as he was that the Lord had enabled him to build a humble temple for Him in Africa, Mr. B. felt that his work was just begun. He commenced holding meetings for public worship every Sabbath, organized a Sabbath-school, and began in regular order the work of an evangelist. But more laborers were needed. If he or Mr. Witt should get sick there was little hope that the other could do the work of the station and care for his sick brother. Besides all this, we should soon want some minister and his wife to come and make their permanent home in Africa. But there was no place for them to live, consequently Mr. B. proceeded forthwith to collect lumber, nails, and paint, and to quarry stone, with which to build a mission residence. In this country it is no great feat to build a house, if one has the money with which to pay expenses; but the building of a decent and substantial house in Africa, and especially at Shengay at that time, was a big undertaking. Mr. B. deserves great credit indeed for his patience and perseverance until this house was completed. He was obliged to bring all his lumber, hardware, and paint from Freetown. Some of the materials were indeed shipped to him by Mr. Flickinger from New York. Stone and sand could be had on the ground, but his masons had to be brought from Freetown, sixty-five miles distant. And such masons! One good stone mason in this country will do as much work as four of them, and do it better. Day by day Mr. B. watched over them, and by dint of effort compelled them to dress the stones somewhat decently. Everything was done at a disadvantage. To obtain lime for mortar he gathered oyster shells and burned them. If some workmen left him he hired others. If a piece of work was not done well he made the workmen do it over again. He thus patiently proceeded day by day, week by week, and month by month till it was finished. It is a substantial stone building with slate roof, of sufficient size (thirty-two by forty feet square) to accommodate a half dozen missionaries with a comfortable home. The "bug-a-bug," so de-

Our Mission House.

structive to wooden buildings, can not destroy it, the storms are not likely to blow it down, so that in all probability when it has stood for fifty years as a home and shelter for missionaries it will be as good and substantial as it was when finished. If he should be able to do nothing else for the Board during the years he might spend in Africa, he had nevertheless accomplished a work that few missionaries would have undertaken, and fewer still persevered in until accomplished.

But so much hard work and the enervating climate began to impair Mr. B.'s health. Being stricken down with fever he would use the best remedies known to the medical profession in Africa, which consisted for the most part of blue mass and quinine, and quinine and blue mass; and as soon as able he would go to work again. Thus he continued to labor alone for a considerable period, begging the Board from time to time to send him reënforcements. Sometimes he would spend a few days in Freetown or at Good Hope station. Once he took a trip to the Teneriffee islands, and in May, 1859, he came to America to recruit his health. He stayed here about nine months, leaving the mission in charge of Rev. John A. Williams.

CHAPTER VI.

Rev J. A. Williams—His Life and Death—Bible-class and Sabbath-school—Two Souls Converted—Their Firmness in the Truth.

I CLOSED the last chapter with a reference to Mr. Williams. I will now introduce the reader to one of the best men and most faithful servants of God whose acquaintance our missionaries were permitted to make in Africa. He was employed by Mr. Bilhiemer as an assistant, in 1859, and continued to serve as such—and sometimes as the only missionary on the ground for months together—*for eleven years.* His Master then took him. And while we thanked God and took courage, as we remembered his humble, faithful life, his zealous labors, his fidelity to the trust reposed in him, and his triumphant death, we yet felt that our mission had sustained a very great loss.

Mr. Williams was a native of Africa, and had been educated in the mission schools of Freetown. He was a local preacher in the

Lady Huntington connection. Prior to entering the service of our mission he was employed as a clerk in a large mercantile establishment in Freetown. He sacrificed his situation and a good salary to enter our service at much lower wages. But he felt he was working for his Master in heaven, and was well repaid in daily supplies of grace. But for the service of this faithful man of God we should probably have no mission in Africa to-day. When our other missionaries were sick or absent from the mission he kept the work going. At one time he was left alone in charge of the mission for about two years. He sustained an excellent character, and exerted a good influence over all the natives with whom he had any connection.

I have already mentioned the fact that Mr. Bilhiemer had organized a Sabbath-school at the mission. About one year after the chapel began to be used he reported a class of ten persons who were seeking the Lord, a part of them in great earnest. Two of them were happily converted to God. One was a young lady named Lucy Caulker, a daughter of the head-man of the town. Though she was quite young and bitterly opposed by her own mother, she yet clung to Jesus with all the ardor of a new-born soul. Like another who was persecuted for righteousness' sake she could sing,

> "Jesus, I my cross have taken
> All to leave and follow thee,
> Naked, poor, despised, forsaken
> Thou from hence my all shalt be."

She was finally compelled to leave the mission. But on Mr. Bilhiemer's return from America to the mission in 1863 he wrote, "Lucy is now here again and seems as much interested in the Sabbath-school and preaching, and is as faithful as ever."

The other convert referred to was a young man who had been taken in at the mission at its very commencement. Of his piety there was no doubt. His earnest prayers, his humble life, his longing desire to know more of the Bible all went to show that he had found the pearl of great price. Mr. Bilhiemer wrote of him in 1863, five years after his conversion: "Tom, one of the young converts who was stolen from the mission by the Purrow Bush Society, has returned, but is not a very good 'Purrow man,' but is greatly attached to the mission and is faithful in duty."

At the time these two souls were converted, in 1858, Mr. B. declared there was a deep religious feeling prevailing among the people. The chapel was crowded with anxious listeners to the word of life from the missionary and Sabbath-school teachers. He was strong in the faith that if his labors had not been interrupted by sickness, or if there had been others at the time to take up and prosecute the work which his failing health forbid his doing, there would have been a general revival.

CHAPTER VII.

Rev. C. O. Wilson—Discouragements—His Return.

BEING well informed as to the uncertain state of Mr. Bilhiemer's health, and well knowing that the mission ought to have an increase in the number of laborers, the Board of Missions earnestly sought men and means for the needed reënforcements. Finally the Rev. C. O. Wilson accepted an appointment, and in September, 1860, he sailed for Africa, arriving at Freetown the 23d of November, having been fifty days at sea. He was agreeably surprised at the kind and brotherly reception given him by the missionaries of Freetown. He remained several days waiting for a boat to convey him to Shengay. He was much impressed with the missionaries and with the native converts. He heard a native preach a sermon in the Episcopal church from the text, "One thing is needful," which he declares would have done credit to the pulpit anywhere. He adds: "While enjoying the means of grace I most forgot that I was in a heathen land; but I was reminded of the fact when I came into the street, by meeting so many of those tall, straight Mohammedans with their greegrees about their necks, and others in a state almost of nudity. There are more than twenty churches in Freetown, yet they have heathens all around them and in their midst unreached by the power of the gospel. Oh, what swarms of people there are in this place! The streets are sometimes teeming as far as the eye can see with human beings, each of whom has an immortal soul, and most of them perhaps strangers to God and without hope in the world, and seem anxious only to supply their few wants here. For this purpose they are incessantly teasing you for something to do. If they see you on the landing it is, 'Massa, you want boat?' 'Captain, got a nice boat; my boat clean.' Or if you have anything in your hand, though it be not more than a pound of rice, it is, 'Massa, I take it for you.' This morning I was visited by one of these job beggars, who accosted me with, 'Massa, you no want servant to do errands and cook?' On telling him I did not, he replied, 'Cause me no got character,' meaning a certificate of good character, a thing which is always required here."

I am sorry to add that Mr. Wilson only remained in Africa a few months. He went to Shengay and stayed a few days, and returned to Freetown on business. Here he was attacked with African fever and confined to his bed for more than a month. On recovering a little his physician advised him by all means to return to America, if he expected to save his life. Mr. Bilhiemer and other missionaries concurring in this opinion, Mr. Wilson felt constrained, though much against his inclination, to follow their advice. Accordingly he returned to America, not having been gone quite a year. He felt very much humiliated that he had been able to do so little for the mission at Shengay. Fearing that the church would be dissatisfied with his course, or that his example might have a bad effect on future missionaries, he generously paid his own passage to and from Africa; and, I am sorry to add, the Board had so little of the grace of generosity or justice as to allow him to do so.

Thus Mr. Bilhiemer was again left with none to assist him but Mr. Williams. His health, too, was still very delicate, yet he was unwilling to leave the mission till some other missionaries should come to take his place. He prayed and waited and suffered long, but none came. It was a dark day for our African mission. For once Mr. B. seems to have been almost overwhelmed. Speaking of Mr. Wilson's return he wrote: "This will be sad news. We owe Mr. Heddle a large amount, and he wants his money. This will be sad news. My own health is precarious. I expect to leave here in April or May. This will be sad news. Will all these things work the abandonment of the African mission? I fear and tremble. God help us. This is a time of great need."

But the wants of the mission caused him to prolong his stay till September, 1861, when he returned to America, having spent five years laboring for the Shengay Mission, and expressing the wish to return to it as soon as he could recruit his health.

CHAPTER VIII.

Sale of Freetown property—Third voyage of Mr. Flickinger—Apathy of the Church—Slave-holders Rebellion.

THE Executive Committee not obtaining a sufficient number of missionaries to man the mission-station properly, and Shengay station proving quite as healthy as Freetown, had no special use for their house in Freetown. It was decided therefore to sell it. This to the committee seemed to be a necessity. There was quite a heavy debt standing against the mission, and the contributions of the church to the missionary treasury were not sufficient to do anything more than meet the current expenses from year to year. Hence they concluded to dispose of the Freetown property to the best advantage.

Now came a new difficulty. As soon as Mr. Bilhiemer learned the wish of the committee he sought and found a purchaser for the house; but owing to the technicalities of English law prevailing in Freetown, a good title it was thought could not be made. Finally the purchaser declined to take the property.

In this state of affairs Mr. Flickinger determined to make a third voyage to Africa. He left Philadelphia in December, 1861, and after a tedious and dangerous voyage reached Goree, the chief town of a French colony about eight hundred miles north of Sierre Leone. Here the vessel put into port and remained two weeks. Thence she sailed down the coast to Gambia, and there tarried two weeks longer. Thus, after a long and perilous voyage across the Atlantic, he was detained from Freetown, at which port he was promised a speedy landing, a whole month. However he reached Freetown at last, and with all speed hastened to Shengay Mission. He found the affairs of the mission in a better condition than he expected. There were several debts however that he had some difficulty in adjusting. But by dint of effort he succeeded in paying the last dollar against the mission, and in making arrangements for Mr. Williams to get along another year without further trouble.

But the main object of his visit was not yet

accomplished. He must sell the Freetown property. He soon found a customer, but, though he had thoroughly equiped himself with a power of attorney in this country, and every qualification he thought necessary to make a deed, if he could only find a buyer when he got there, Freetown lawyers and judges would accept no title that he could make. However he found a customer and sold the house for $2,250.00, and was assured that a deed signed by all the members of the Executive Committee would be satisfactory. The deed was prepared, sent to this country, signed by the committee and returned to the purchaser. And thus ends the history of the Freetown mission house.

The main mission building, referred to in a former chapter, not being finished yet, and there not being sufficient room to accommodate him and Mr. Williams and his family, he determined to return home as soon as practicable. He was the more anxious to return by reason of the terrible war going on in this country, and the news that was circulated in all the colonies of Sierre Leone that England had declared war against the United States. From these and other considerations not necessary here to mention, he sailed for America, and arrived safely in Dayton early in April, 1862.

Fearing that some of the church members who did not understand the state of affairs as well as they might would take offense, or charge him with spending money unnecessarily, Mr. F. generously paid his own expenses, amounting in the aggregate to over two hundred dollars. For this sacrifice of suffering, and peril, and money the Board of Missions returned him a vote of thanks!

It will thus be seen how Mr. Flickinger has labored and spent money to establish and perpetuate the mission in Africa. Had the whole church been as enthusiastic in its prosecution it would soon have been abundantly supplied with missionaries and means to make it a power for good in the midst of the works of darkness by which it is surrounded. But it appeared to be necessary that somebody should go before, show the importance and practicability of the undertaking, and thus, like John the Baptist, prepare the people for the work.

But there was a cause for this apathy toward the African mission, and I should be unfaithful to my convictions if I omitted the mention of it. There was war at home; and such a war as afflicted every household. The slave-holders' rebellion had put the life of the nation in jeopardy. There was scarcely a family that did not count some of its members absent engaged in the work of suppressing this gigantic insurrection. Their thoughts, their sympathies, their prayers, their money were all engaged in this life and death struggle of the nation.

Now, it is not in the nature of things that an individual or a nation can be so intensely absorbed in two things at one time. Farmers neglected their crops, mechanics their shops, merchants their stores, lawyers and doctors their professions; and it is not strange that the United Brethren Church somewhat neglected her African mission, while the nation was passing through this fiery ordeal.

The Church was largely engaged, moreover, during these years in feeding, clothing, educating, and preaching the gospel to the colored people of the southern states, who had recently been made free men by Abraham Lincoln's proclamation of emancipation. While therefore I admit that the Church was rather neglectful of her foreign mission during these four eventful years, there is some apology in the alacrity with which she assumed and discharged the immense responsibilities so suddenly and unexpectedly thrown upon her by the slave-holders rebellion against the very existence of the nation.

CHAPTER IX.

Mr. Bilhiemer's visit to America—Marriage—Returns to
Africa—Joy of the people—God's approval.

COMMITTING the care of the mission to that faithful man of God, Mr. Williams, Mr. Bilhiemer returned to America for the tripple purpose—whether he was conscious of all these purposes at the time I can not say, but but so it turned out—of recruiting his health, stirring up the zeal of the Church on the missionary question, and marrying a wife. He remained in this country nearly a year, and spent the time visiting annual conferences and holding special missionary meetings, instructing the people on the wants of the heathen in Africa, and encouraging them to hope and labor for their conversion; and, as we intimated in a former chapter, such encouragement was never more necessary. The people needed stirring. By his lectures, his prayers, and the exhibition of curiosities brought from Africa, among which were found "certain strange gods," he awakened the people somewhat to a sense of duty. Meantime his health slowly improved, and after wedding Miss Amanda L. Hanby, daughter of Ex-bishop Hanby, he again sailed for Africa early in September, 1862. His wife was a well educated, deeply pious young lady, and as thoroughly imbued with the missionary spirit as himself.

When it was known that he and his wife had consecrated themselves to the Shengay Mission many of the ministers and members of the Church rejoiced, took courage, and renewed their devotion to the prosecution of that work.

When the Board met the next spring they passed a resolution assuring them of their hearty sympathy and coöperation, and pledging them "a support to the uttermost cent their resources would allow." And the Board reflected the sentiments of nearly the whole church whose missionary operations they were managing.

If there was increased hope and faith in the Church at home, there was gladness and joy, I might say unbounded enthusiasm, among the people of Shengay when Mr. and Mrs.

Bilhiemer arrived at the station. The natives could not restrain themselves. They knew not how to manifest their gladness. If one had come to them from the dead they could not have been more overjoyed. Mr. Bilhiemer wrote: "Mr. Williams, the scholars, and nearly all the people met us at the wharf. We had a fine time shaking hands. There were at least a half dozen hands extended at once. The people seem greatly rejoiced over my return, but more especially are they pleased "wid de fine misses." We have had visitors nearly every day. We are thankful the people are so kindly disposed toward us. I feared lest I should not find things all right here; to my astonishment I find them in a much better condition than I expected."

At the same time Mrs. Bilhiemer wrote: "As Mr. Bilhiemer is too busy to write about the little things that would interest you, I would do a little. King Caulker is very sick (cause, rum), and his son Stephen also, the latter once a professor of religion, and is still the best among them. I think his afflictions may be the means of bringing him back to God.

"You may remember Ribbon, the lame

fisher boy. He has been sick for more than a month, with little hope of recovery, and should he die I think his soul would be at rest. I shall never forget with what earnestness and delight he grasped the thought that Christ died for all men. 'Yes, sir,' said he, 'he died for black man as well as white man. He done die for me own self all the same like one white man.' I hope soon to organize a class of women to teach reading, sewing, anything that will make an opportunity to tell them about the blessed Jesus."

I make these quotations to show that they went not only to a large but a ripe field. Preachers are not often received with more enthusiasm in Christian churches in America. Now, why were the poor heathen rejoiced to see these missionaries coming? It was not the hope of gain, or honor, or pleasure, but because they felt their need of instruction in divine truth and believed the missionaries could impart it. If the preparations that Cornelius had made to receive the Apostle Peter, and the eagerness of himself and the whole company assembled to "hear words whereby they might be saved," was the divine approval to Peter that he had gone to the right place to preach Jesus and the resurrection, which he proceeded immediately to do, how much more ought the United Brethren Church believe, when she considers how overjoyed the poor Africans were to see the messenger of the cross setting foot on their soil, that God had called them to this work? Why should any have hesitated? Yet at this very period there was a sharp controversy carried on in the *Religious Telescope*, between old and well tried ministers of the Church, as to whether it was our duty to send missionaries to Africa! Tell it not in Gath!

"How beautiful are the feet of them that preach the gospel of peace, and bring glad tidings of good things!" There is every reason to believe that the Africans, in no small numbers, from first to last, have received our missionaries most gladly, not for their own sakes merely, but because they were the messengers of God, come to proclaim to them life and salvation. It was the message they bore that made their feet beautiful in the eyes of them who had always sat in the darkness of death. With such proofs of God's approval the Church should never falter in the prosecution of the Sherbro Mission.

CHAPTER X.

Climate—Seasons—Sickness.

HAVING so often alluded to the sickness of our missionaries I will now give my readers an account of the climate and seasons of Africa. The continent of Africa is very large. Of the five great natural divisions of the globe Africa is second in size. Asia, the largest, has sixteen millions of square miles; Europe, the smallest, three and a half millions; North America, eight millions; South America, seven millions; Africa, eleven millions of square miles. Nearly all of this vast continent lies in the Torrid Zone, and has therefore a much warmer climate than any of the other grand divisions of the globe. The average temperature at Shengay and Freetown is about eighty-six degrees, which is nearly equal to our hottest weather in this country. But as the days and nights are almost equal the year round the heat is not so oppressive as might be supposed. The longest days at the mission are not quite twelve hours and a half, and the shortest days about eleven and a half hours. Hence you see their days and nights, as to their length, are about like ours in March and September. Like it is here, the nights are cooler than the days. In fact they never have such hot nights as we often have in June, when the days are sixteen, and the nights only eight hours in length. The nights are always cool in Africa, the days always warm. This continued warm weather makes the people lazy. They do not feel like work, and it makes no difference whether they have thick dresses, thin dresses, or no dresses at all. When June with its teeming showers, singing birds, and glowing foliage and flowers smiles upon them they have no fear or care for January. They know it will be as warm as June, and do not trouble themselves to procure much clothing or build warm houses. A mere shanty, or no shelter at all will do, so they think; and thus thousands of them eat, and sleep, and die without apparently rising much higher in the scale of human beings than the beasts that perish.

They do not there, as here, speak of spring, summer, autumn, and winter; for although they have the same months it is not the same kind of weather. They have but two seasons, a dry and a rainy one. They have from seven to eight months without any rain at all, and then four or five months of rainy weather. These rainy seasons commence with violent tornados, and close up in much the same way. The most piercing and vivid lightning and the most terrific thunder, accompanied with violent, sweeping winds, such as we seldom witness here, are as sure to visit the western coast of Africa as the months continue to come and go. After a few days, however, these storms of wind cease, and then the rainy season becomes, to Americans especially, even more pleasant than the dry season, because it is considerably cooler. Were it not much more sickly than the dry, it would be the more delightful season of the two. For the reader must understand it does not rain all the time. Far from it. Sometimes a rain will continue to fall incessantly for a day and a half, but it generally ceases in about twelve hours, Then they will have from one to three days of beautiful, clear weather, and after that another rain, till toward the close of the rainy season, when they will have some more violent tornadoes. After these have passed the dry season returns, and they have no more rain for about eight months; but, in the absence of rain, they have heavy dews, so that it does not become so dry as many would suppose.

This continual warm weather keeps the forests always green. The leaves are always falling and always forming, so that there is no perceptible difference from one month to another. The savannas, or prairies as we would call them, are always green, birds always sing, flowers always bloom, and fruits, and grains, and vegetables are always maturing. No frosts to wither anything. It is perpetual spring. How delightful!

But there is no rose without its thorn. This continued wet weather of the rainy season, heat of all seasons, the extensive swamps that abound on the coast, and the matchless growth and decay of vegetable matter are the sources of a great deal of sickness among the people. This sickness is caused by the malaria or poison arising from the decay of vegetation. It is the same kind of poison and the same kind of sickness that we have in this country, but it is far worse. We here have ague and billious fever. There they are taken with a chill or shake, and this will be followed with high fever, continuing several hours, when it goes off, and the patient may feel quite well till the next chill draws on, which will be more severe, and, if he be a foreigner, he may die in a few days, or the fever may continue for weeks and even months before he dies, or, after passing through a protracted period of suffering, he may recover, if he has a good constitution and is properly treated by his physician. The natives suffer much from these malarial diseases, though they fare much better than strangers before they are thoroughly acclimated. Yet people live and die in Africa, after all, much as in every other country. Sickness prevails more or less everywhere in this world, and death, by one cause or another, comes to all. If the forests were cleared, the swamps drained, and the habits of the people improved, as in this and other civilized countries, I have no doubt that the healthfulness of Africa would be greatly increased. If the gospel be once heartily embraced by the great body of the people, we may reasonably expect that the natural resources of the country, more numerous and extensive perhaps than any other on the globe, will be fully developed. Thus while the gospel will save their souls in heaven it will also greatly bless them, as it has us, soul and body, in this world.

CHAPTER XI.

Religion—Superstition—The gospel their only hope.

SO far as known the Africans all have some ideas of religion and all worship something. The Mandingoes (book-men), and many others are Mohammedans. They profess to believe in the true God, but they have very crude notions of the character and will of God, and they deny entirely the redemption of the world by Jesus Christ. Indeed the great majority of those who accept the religion of Mohammet know nothing of the name of Jesus, and what they call religion serves only to confuse the mind and prevent them from accepting the truth as it is in Jesus. These Mohammedans are as ignorant, selfish, and superstitious as the grosser heathen. In fact their thoughts and superstitions seem to pervade the whole population to a greater or less degree. They attach great weight to charms, signs, greegrees, and the like. A greegree is from one to six inches square, made of two or three thicknesses of stiff leather sewed together, and containing a few letters or sentences of Arabic writing. These they carry about their persons. One greegree is supposed to keep off diseases, another wild animals, and a third to prevent national calamities, such as war, pestilence, and famine. They have so much faith in these greegrees and reverence for them that it amounts to idolatry. If they worship anything they worship the greegrees.

Others worship the devil. They think he has the control of the world, and that the everlasting destiny of men is committed to him. True, they suppose that there is a great God, the first cause of all things, but they believe that men are so ignorant, polluted, and worthless that God takes no notice of them. He is so exalted and with all so busy in other matters that he does not concern himself about the wants or worship of human beings. Hence they turn to the devil. They build houses to worship him in, some for public and others for private use. They sacrifice to him, cook victuals and put in his houses, and verily believe that his Satanic majesty comes and eats up what they take him! Of course they become more and more like the being whom they worship.

Still others make images or statues of stone, iron, lead, wood, or anything that they imagine will answer the purpose. These are usually of the crudest workmanship. The specimens our missionaries have brought to this country are hideous looking things. Yet the poor deluded heathen bow to them and worship them, believing there will come to them some good, some praise, or honor, or good luck, on account of the service they have rendered the gods, for none are satisfied with one god. They have gods many and lords many. They are not very particular what they worship. Many worship the earth, saying they believe it to be the wife of God! Some worship serpents, creeping things, four footed beasts, fowls of the air, the stars of heaven, everything and anything but the true God! One of the church missionaries from England says he saw a crowd of people assembled "offering sacrifices to a common ball and three decanter stoppers, recommending themselves and their children to the favor of that evil spirit of whom the ball and stoppers were the representatives. They say, like the Roman Catholics of the pictures, that when they address the ball and glass stopper they speak not to them, but to the devil that lives in the bush" (woods).

This state of ignorance and superstition has continued for thousands of years. The children learn nothing better from their parents, and until some people who are instructed in the way of life through Jesus Christ go and preach the gospel to them there is no hope that they will come to any better state for thousands of years to come. But will the gospel better their condition? Certainly it will. If any doubt, let them look at England, France, Germany, any Christian country, and let them consider that they all and each were once as ignorant, superstitious, selfish and idolatrous, within the period recorded by reliable historians, as are the negroes of west Africa to-day. Their degradation, then, instead of causing them to be a hissing and by word, should stir the depths of our souls with emotions akin to those which moved the Lord Jesus to come into the world, and in due time to die for the ungodly. Just as man has demonstrated by thousands of years of degradation his incapacity to rise out of his idolatrous state of himself, the gospel has proved itself thousands of times to be a sovereign balm for all the ills that afflict humanity.

CHAPTER XII.

Agriculture—Horticulture.

THERE is, perhaps, no country in the world where the soil and climate are so favorable for the farmer and fruit grower. But the natives know nothing about tilling the soil. Rice is the chief crop. This they scatter about over the ground without any previous plowing or preparation of any kind, and then scratch the ground a little with a hoe. Nothing more is done till harvest, about four months from the time of sowing. Then they send some of the old people and children out of the town (all of the Africans live in towns) to lodge in some miserable hut about the middle of the rice field, to chase away the vast flocks of rice birds that now appear to devour the crop. They cut off the stalks close to the ground, tie them up in small bundles or sheaves, and lay them on stumps and stones to dry for threshing. They frequently raise two crops of rice a year on the same piece of land.

Cotton grows luxuriously. It is a natural product of the soil. They raise two crops a year from the same land. They also raise coffee, but they pay little attention to it as yet. One tree at Monrovia, the capital of Liberia, is reported to have yielded thirty pounds at a single gathering. If the natives could be induced to clear their lands, lay them off in small farms and properly cultivate these three products, rice, cotton, and coffee, it would enable them to live in a state of ease and elegance unknown to any other farmers in the world. But this is not all. Sugar cane grows almost spontaneously. There is probably no country in the world where sugar cane is more easily cultivated, or yields a better crop, either as to quantity or quality. Then they have cam wood in unlimited quantities. Red wood, bar wood, and other dyes also abound.

Palm oil is abundant. This oil is procured from the dates that grow on the palm-trees. The people live chiefly on rice and palm oil. Palm oil is used with many articles of diet. It is to the African what butter is to the American. The palm-tree, moreover, is perhaps the most useful tree in their forests.

The inner bark is manufactured into a thick cloth. The leaves form an excellent thatch, or roof for houses. From the outer bark they manufacture baskets, mats, &c. Besides the oil derived from dates, it is proper to add that the dates themselves, which are nearly as large as hens' eggs, are esteemed a great luxury. Indian corn, wherever it is cultivated, yields abundantly. This of itself will some day be a great source of wealth.

As to fruits, there is a great variety and an endless supply. Figs, olives, pine apples, oranges, cocoa nuts, lemons, bananas, grapes, plums, and many more varieties. But the people pay little attention to growing fruit. What mother earth brings forth of herself they use without striving to increase the quantity or improve the quality.

In addition to all this there is probably no country richer in its mineral resources. The country is well watered, well supplied with stone, and every material that is needed in the highest state of civilization.

With such a wealth of natural resources this ought to be one of the most delightful countries in the world. Such it will become if the people can be lifted out of their state of barbarism. And as they are begging the Christian people of other countries to come and teach them, we may be sure their redemption draweth nigh.

CHAPTER XIII.

Sickness of missionaries—Mr. Bilhiemer's final return to America—Mr. Williams alone—Prospects.

IT was now thought by the Board that the mission would soon be in a flourishing condition. Mr. Bilhiemer and his wife, and Mr. Williams and his wife were all employed. This was believed to be the Lord's time to favor our Zion. But, alas, for human expectation! Mr. Bilhiemer had scarcely gone to work before the African fever, which he had fondly hoped had been entirely removed by the few months stay which he had enjoyed in America, returned and soon quite prostrated him. Mrs. Bilhiemer was also attacked with fever, and as months wore away there were few days when they were both able to be up and at work. One or the other was sick nearly all the time. Sometimes neither was able to help the other. And to make the matter still worse, Mr. Williams and his family suffered much affliction also. In the hope of improving their health, Mr. Williams removed to Freetown, and continued there, from time to time, most of the period Mr. Bilhiemer remained at the mission. They strove hard to have regular prayers morning and evening at the mission, to teach a day school, a Sabbath-school, and to have preaching every Sabbath. Their hearts and hopes alike prompted them to undertake much, but their strength failed. Their labors were often interrupted. At times they could do little more than suffer for Christ's sake. This indeed was a great deal, and they felt entirely willing to suffer, but they well knew that this would not teach the people the way of life. At this time Mr. Bilhiemer wrote:

"The rainy season is now nearly past, and we have had a wet and unhealthy time. Both Mrs. Bilhiemer and myself have suffered much within the past five months. I was kept indoors for weeks together, and for nearly five weeks I was unable to have family worship. Mrs. Bilhiemer was not out of the house for three months. Mr. Williams was also ill, and in Freetown from June to August. The change of season has brought a change of feeling for the better in me."

But Mr. Bilhiemer seems soon to have become thoroughly convinced that his work in Africa was about done, and commenced to urge the Board to send reënforcements, telling them that he would shortly have to leave Africa. He thought it useless to remain there when he could not work, and he had no hope of recovering his health if he remained. The Board heard, but hoped even against hope that Mr. Bilhiemer's health would improve, and that he would remain. "The wish was father to the thought." The people of this country were engaged, from the greatest to the least, in the heat and strife and suffering of a great national war, and the Board, as before mentioned, had new and unexpected openings for missionary labor; and these openings were such as could not be neglected or postponed. Hence they employed a number of missionaries and teachers to labor among the thousands of freedmen whose fetters had been just broken off by the Union army. Such was the din and strife and anxiety of the time that the Church had its attention partially drawn away from Africa. Meantime Mr. and Mrs. Bilhiemer, again committing the charge of the mission to Mr. Williams, sailed for America, arriving at home about the first of May, 1864. They were both quite feeble, and suffered much after their return, but finally regained their wonted health.

Mr. Bilhiemer had now spent seven years in the prosecution of this mission; and though he sometimes became discouraged with the Board, the Church, and with himself, he never for a moment doubted that with faithful, persevering labor the United Brethren Church would yet be successful in bringing many of the sons and daughters of benighted Africa to Jesus Christ. It was a sore trial to part from the mission, but such was the reduced state of his constitution that he was obliged finally to relinquish all hope of ever returning to Shengay Station as a missionary.

Mr. Williams now removed to the station and renewed his devotion to the mission. The Board failed to send him any assistance for some time, but trusting in the Lord he labored on, prayed, and quietly waited for the salvation of God. Nor did he labor or hope in vain. He had the pleasure—the greatest delight of the faithful preacher of the gospel—of seeing the people awaking up out of their stupor, and inquiring after salvation. He wrote the corresponding secretary a letter a few months after Mr. Bilhiemer's return to America, which so well reflects the character and labors of the man, as well as the condition and prospects of our work, that I give it entire.

"Freetown, Sierre Leone, Oct. 20, 1864.

"Reverend and Dear Sir:—Your letters were duly received on the 17th day of August, and I must acknowledge that they were like life put into a dead body to me. I wrote to Bro. Bilhiemer in June, and had never received an answer till the above date, when both of your letters were handed to me by Brother Whiton, from Booth, on his way to town. I read them not only to myself, but to the people. All that were present that day in the chapel seemed to be well pleased.

"It is always encouraging to us when we receive letters from you, especially to learn that the Christians are praying for us, which is indeed cheering. May the good Lord hear those prayers, and open the windows of heaven and rain down his blessings in abundance on this part of the vineyard. Dear brother, if we look at the work of laboring in Africa, viewing it from a human stand-point exclusively, it seems a hopeless task, but I believe God's word is a pledge for it, for God has spoken good things concerning Zion in Africa, even Shengay, as well as elsewhere, and I trust the day draweth nigh when it shall be redeemed. I look forward with joy and ardent hope that the morning will dawn.

"Permit your servant to ask the young Christians in the churches this simple question, 'Why don't you come over and preach the gospel to poor perishing souls in obedience to our Master's great command?' Are they afraid of the fever? Do they forget the promise? Has he not promised to go with his heralds even to the end? I will do my best depending on him. I am longing for the time when I shall be able to speak the language freely. Then I will tell them more of Jesus. At present I can only impart instruction to those few who can understand me, but I trust the time will soon come when I will be able to go from village to village, sowing or scattering the seed of the gospel.

"You are aware that I have no interpreter. The first Sabbath of October, as I was preaching in the barry, Mr. George Caulker offered his services as an interpreter. The country people were astonished at this, for he was a young man that never attended or came near where the word of God is preached. At the conclusion of the meeting I was obliged to exclaim, "What hath God wrought!"

At another time he wrote: "I am in favor of holding meetings on Sabbath at Shengay town barry, (court-house), for there you can get all the slaves as well as the freedmen to attend; but they seem afraid to come to the chapel, though I do not think they are prevented by their owners. I have held a number of meetings there during the past year. I am glad to announce that many of the natives begin to see the foolishness of their devil-worship. I am also happy to state that the Sabbath is well observed by the natives of Shengay. If a stranger should happen to put a shore there on Sunday he would at once know, without being told, that it was the Lord's day."

Time passed. The Board sought more laborers, but they were hard to find. Some promised to go after a while; others were willing to go if they felt it to be their duty to go, and so on to the end of the chapter of excuses. In the mean time a number of persons accepted appointments from the Board for that field, among whom may be named, Prof. W. T. Jackson, Rev. R. West, Rev. W. O. Grimm, but for one reason or another neither of them ever went, so that Brother Williams was left to manage the mission as best he could alone.

CHAPTER XIV.

Mr. and Mrs. Hadley—Arrival in Africa—Difficulty of reaching the heathen—Meeting of the Board.

BUT these delays and discouragements did not dishearten the Church. The war had closed. The freedmen were engaging the sympathy and moral and material support of all the churches in America. All seemed to feel that Africa had come to our doors. In this state of things the United Brethren Church very justly concluded that while she might palliate her feeble efforts in Africa by the help she had rendered the freedmen, she could not justify the giving up of that mission on any grounds whatsoever. We had gone too far to think of retreating. The work must go on.

The Board therefore resolved to increase its efforts to carry forward the work already begun. In response to a call made by the Executive Committee, the Rev. O. Hadley, of the St. Joseph Conference, answered, "Here am I; send me," and his amiable and zealous Christian wife answered, "Even so; send us." Of course so excellent a man and minister as Mr. Hadley was known to be, was appointed at the earliest convenience of the committee. Without ceremony or delay they went to New York, and on the 22d of October, 1866, they sailed for Africa. After a tedious voyage of forty-five days—twenty days longer than was expected—and much sea sickness, they landed at Freetown. Of this sickness Mr. Hadley good humoredly says: "We tried to frown it down for a time, but saw that it was useless, and then 'turned in' and tamely submitted to our fate. Well it gave us a terrible round. Others have spoken of it as a ludicrous, harmless disease; but that was not the kind we had. I am of the opinion that after any one has had such an acquaintance with it as we have, he will have a degree of respect for it, if no affection."

After describing the condition of the mission property and surrounding scenery, Mr. Hadley continues: "I never can be satisfied till I see some of our people soundly converted to Christ. We feel that the Lord is with us. About thirty or forty persons attend services on Sabbath. We have had some three applications by parents or friends for us to take children to school, but we are not prepared for this yet."

Mr. Hadley, like all his predecessors, on looking round and seeing how much there was to do, and the urgent need of its being soon done, and considering the resources of the church at home, was filled with amazement. Why the Board, prompted by the prayers and contributions of the Church, could help sending more missionaries, was to him a mystery. The following quotation is from his second letter:

"Our morning and evening prayers have in attendance about fifteen or twenty persons, and our Sabbath services about double that number. I have preached once at Shengay. I had quite a good congregation, and felt that I was doing good. But I am grieved that we can not get at the *poor* people. There are scarcely any children attending our day-school but the Caulker family. Some of the poor slaves seem to think that the benefits of the mission are designed for this family, and they themselves seemed to think that when I came their children would be fed, clothed.

and educated by the mission. We have been visited by the old man and most of the family. The old man was quite sensible and inclined to talk of religion, but many of the others, I think, are only running after presents. But they have learned generally that I did not come to make presents and help them temporally. Why, sir, one of the dignitaries of this family, who lives some distance from here, said he did not want the missionaries to come into his part of the country, as *all* the people would then become *smart*. Do you see? The very same hydra-headed, cloven-footed, pro-slavery demon which tried to rule America. But I believe that God will make the truth and the right prevail here as he has there. These are the Pharisees of this country, who stand in the door of the kingdom and prevent them from going in who would.

"Oh, if I could only speak the Sherbro tongue, so that I could go into the hovels of the poor and teach them of Christ, how great would be the door opened to do good! But we are constrained to think that Christ is with us. Some of our men are serious, and I am praying every day for their conversion.

I want the tongue of a new convert to preach Christ all around here, and stir up the dry bones. I think Satan is out of humor, and therefore am encouraged in the Lord. There is a large field opened, and plenty of work to do, it we are only prepared to do it."

It will be seen by these extracts that Mr. Hadley had both the head and heart of a missionary. He comprehended the situation at a glance, and he impressed himself on the natives as one who had come to them for a great and good purpose. Perhaps there never was a man more fully consecrated to the cause of missions than was Mr. Hadley.

These stirring words from our missionaries had a good effect in the Church. They did much to overcome prejudice and remove opposition that existed in the minds of some of the members of the Church. When the Board met in May, 1867, it was resolved to build a new chapel as soon as possible, and renew our devotion to that work. Pending the adoption of this resolution Mr. Flickinger, the corresponding secretary, said: "I am perplexed; I never had a doubt of the propriety of its commencement; I am confident that God in his providence favored its location; but, in view of existing difficulties, I sometimes think it would be well to step aside and let some one else take the work in hand, and do with it as seemeth best. We have a good location in Africa—one of the best on the whole coast. It is just on the borders of civilization. But there are some good men in the Church who are opposed to it, and are exerting their influence against it. In view of this it is hard to proceed; and yet we have never given the African mission a fair trial. It is a wonder we have succeeded even as well as we have. Not until we have given it a fair trial can I consent to its discontinuance."

Mr. Kemp said "the African mission had given the Church about all the missionary zeal it ever had. He was determined not to be discouraged. He had heard many disparaging remarks from sources from whence we should expect better things. One brother complained that our missionary had spent two hundred dollars going to Teneriffe Island to recruit his health! He felt that the Church needed a fresh baptism of the Holy Spirit to enable her to prosecute the work, both home and foreign, with greater vigor."

CHAPTER XV.

Mr. Hadley's first year—Strong faith—Discouragements—
Mohammedans.

DURING the first year of their stay in Africa Mr. Hadley was afflicted a considerable portion of the time, yet he was cheerful and hopeful. As the tornadoes of the second rainy season announced that another dry season was drawing on, and another season for successful missionary labor, his heart was cheered with the prospect that loomed up before him. His religious experience was ripened and deepened by the acclimating process through which he had passed, his understanding of the wants of the heathen better informed, and his conviction of the duty of those who loved God to impart the gospel to the poor heathen fully confirmed. As yet, it is true, he could not see the work of his hands prospering. To his senses the scene was dark indeed, but he had faith in God. His soul was stayed on

God. Underneath him were the everlasting arms. With such a conviction, with such a trust, with such implicit faith, he seems to have been one of the happiest of men. Some of his utterances make one think of Martin Luther and John Knox. True, his surroundings and trials were different from theirs; but, like them, he felt that his only help, his only source of success, was in God. But he had not the shadow of a doubt that God would cause the seed sown in Africa to spring up in many hearts unto everlasting life. The following extracts from letters written to the corresponding secretary will show the fulness and richness of his personal experience, and the strength of his faith in the ultimate triumph of the gospel:

"The Lord turns everything to our spiritual good while in the way of duty.

"Tell our friends that their prayers for us are not lost. We are contented and quite happy. We fear not the climate, nor sickness, nor death.

"The low estate (more properly, the desperate condition,) of the surrounding heathen calls more loudly for help. Our race has been active for years in the degradation of Africa.

If we wish our skirts clear of her blood, let us be more active in her exaltation.

"Because Satan has his seat here, shall we faint and give up the contest, and go home like cowards, leaving all the vast field to him? Where is the man who says yes? Who shall stop to count numbers or weigh money against the souls of the heathen? Let him make himself known. Let him oppose with knowledge that the work shall be done. If *we* refuse, others will not. I am not able to see far, nor say much, but I can not persuade my soul that this work is to fail."

At another time he wrote: "My soul is troubled for this work. It is before me and upon my heart night and day. Surely this travail is from above, and so not in vain. I am astonished and perplexed, but by no means in despair. If it please the Lord that I die without seeing a single soul converted, I am determined not to doubt but to die in the faith of the final triumph of the gospel in this country. I have made up my mind to believe against the seeing of my eyes and the hearing of my ears, when Christ authorizes me to do so. Oh, that this same Jesus Christ who loved us unto death, may pity these poor heathen, and also us whom he hath sent. Bro. F., I can not say a word, I feel like I do not know anything about this matter, only I believe the Lord has sent us. It may be more enthusiasm than I am aware of, but it does not die out."

At this time Mr. Hadley spoke fully of the impediments that lay in the way of evangelizing Africa. Slavery prevailed to an alarming extent. Slave owners there, as everywhere else, knew if their slaves were once enlightened they could no longer hold them. An enlightened people can not be enslaved. Hence these slave owners always oppose the efforts of the missionaries. Mr. Hadley said they prevented him from having any access to a great many of the poor heathen. He felt burdened when he thought of their wretched, ignorant, dying condition, and of the compassion of Jesus toward them. His soul yearned to do something for them. But alas! more than half of the people in that part of Africa were slaves, and their masters stood between them and the gospel.

Polygamy was another source of trouble. Many men in Africa had all the wives they could obtain. This was soul-destroying. It degraded women to a level with the brutes. They were called wives, but slaves would have been a more appropriate title. As soon as a man obtained three or four wives he thought he was able to live without any further effort on his part. His wives did the hard work, and he enjoyed the labor of their hands. Of course the gospel would tolerate none of this, and it everywhere met the stern and steadfast opposition of every man who had more than one wife.

The Mohammedans were another source of opposition. They could read, and because they had "book-palaver," the people did not readily distinguish between them and the missionary of the cross. These Mohammedans would not condemn anything that would displease the Africans. They allowed slavery, allowed and practiced polygamy, used charms, greegrees, and every foolish and hateful thing common to the heathen. Hence it was easy for them to make the people believe that the Christian missionaries would take away their liberty, make cruel exactions, and forever destroy their happiness. There are many even in Christian lands who will not make the self-denial necessary to become Christians.

What wonder, then, if the heathen, having such blind and deceptive leaders as the Mohammedans, should hesitate to accept the gospel? Sense outweighs faith with all the children of this world. This is doubly so in heathen countries. The people know and care little about restraining their passions. They are led captive by the devil at his will. How sad their condition!

As these Mohammedans are numerous, and exert a great influence over so many millions of the people in Africa, I must add that they are without natural affection as to their female children, and thus make the heathen, whose habitations are already full of cruelty, worse instead of better. A missionary once asked a gray-haired Moslem—a man professing the religion of Mohammed—how many children he had. He replied, "I have no children at all." The man then asked, "Whose daughters are those whom I saw running across the court?" "Oh," said he, "those are mine, but *they are nothing but girls.*" He asked another how many children he had. He replied, with an air of triumph, "I have four sons, but praise to God, I have no daughters."

Thus it will be seen that the little half-starved, half naked—and thousands of them entirely nude—children of Africa are to be made more miserable by the teaching and practice of these blind leaders of the blind. No wonder Mr. Hadley's soul was so troubled when he looked upon this sad picture of humanity.

CHAPTER XVI.

Day and Sabbath-schools—War—Mr. and Mrs. Hadley return to America—His death.

THE work of teaching, preaching, and praying still went on. Our missionaries reported in 1868 that they had twenty scholars in the day-school. Most of these were members of the Caulker family. If a few others were brought in, they would remain but a short time. For one cause or another, sometimes known to the missionaries, but often entirely unknown, these other scholars would disappear, and that would be the last they would see of them; but they secretly believed that King Caulker had something to do in sending them away.

But the Sabbath-school was more hopeful. There were twice as many persons in attendance, and they came more regularly than the day scholars, took a deeper interest in the instruction they received, and, on the whole, as is often the case in long established churches in this country, the Sabbath-school was the most hopeful feature of the mission. The old people were so confirmed in their habits of thought and attachment to heathen practices, that there was little hope of their conversion. "Can the Ethiopian change his skin, or the leopard his spots?" But they might cherish a good hope that these little children, being so early taught the name and love of Jesus, would, as they came to years, not only forsake the idols and wicked practices of the generations preceding them, but serve as agents to win their countrymen from the ways of sin.

Of this school Mr. Hadley wrote, July, 1868: "Our Sabbath-school is more interesting. This is due principally to the distribution of reward tickets and books for the memorizing of the Scriptures. We have one officer, three teachers, and twenty-four scholars. Verses of Scripture memorized and repeated, five thousand one hundred and thirty-two. Six of our best scholars have repeated three thousand five hundred and seventy-five of these. The Sabbath-school superintendents in America can tell how this will compare with their schools. Our prayer-meetings, on Tuesday evening, and Bible class have been very good. Five persons whom we had greatly hoped to see converted soon are for the present apparently out of our reach, but another one has lately given evidence of distress on account of sin. We rejoice at every indication that the Holy Spirit is working in the dark hearts about us. We may, perhaps, encourage ourselves too soon; but we hope that it may please the Lord to bring about a great change for the better in this place."

Notwithstanding Mr. Hadley's faith and hope he was doomed to disappointment. Though his health at the beginning of his second year was improved, and the prospect for usefulness much brighter than at the beginning of the first year, it was only apparent. A deadly disease had laid its seductive hand upon him. Consumption was slowly undermining his life. But he was so engaged in the work in hand he almost forgot himself. The zeal of the Lord's house literally ate him up. After his second year was half gone his faithful wife wrote: "Nothing very serious troubles me, but Mr. Hadley has some fever, and his cough and throat have gradually become more irritated and troublesome. Ulceration seems to be going on speedily. I use such remedies as are at hand, but they fail to profit as before. Still, I trust, the Lord may deliver him as at other times. It seems that his labors in Africa may soon have an end. He may be able to begin the buildings, but I do not think he can finish them."

The buildings spoken of by Mrs. Hadley had reference to a new chapel and some out buildings for the use of the mission. He undertook the new chapel. Men were employed to quarry and dress the stone; but before the work proceeded very far the cry of war put everything into confusion and uncertainty; and before the excitement of a war subsided the rainy season drew on, and Mr. Hadley's health becoming still worse the work was allowed to cease altogether.

Yielding to necessity, after two and a half years of labor in Africa, Mr. Hadley and his wife returned to America. He had now become entirely unable to labor any more, and Mrs. Hadley could do little more than take care of her husband. Finally they committed the mission to Mr. Williams, under God, and sailed for America. They arrived in Dayton,

Ohio, April 15, 1869. Mr. Hadley was in a dying condition. He could say very little about the mission or anything else. In a short time they proceeded to their home near Lafayette, Indiana, and in a few days after Mrs. Hadley wrote to Mr. Flickinger the following interesting, sad, and yet cheering, letter:

"May 4th, 1869.

"Bro. F.:—Some of us have parted to meet no more on the shores of time. My dear companion failed in strength and breath so fast that he only survived a few days after reaching home. He was entirely sensible of his suffering, and knew us to the last. He said in his last hours that I should not shed tears for him, and that he would soon land where he would never want for breath, and, 'Come, O my Savior! and tarry not.' He struggled hard with death, and just as day dawned on the 28th of April, his eyes were closed to this world; and at ten o'clock A. M., on the 29th, his dear body was carried to the chapel, a discourse was preached by Rev. A. W. Wainscott, and then we looked upon the pale form once more, and saw it quietly laid to rest in its narrow home until the resurrection morn.

"I only ask for grace to help me to continue in the same precious faith my dear husband had in his Savior. We never lamented that we had forsaken all for Christ's sake and the gospel's. We only regretted that we did not suffer more willingly.

"How short is life, and yet how great the work. Oh, who can die without Jesus! Precious Savior! Oh, that I may love him with all my heart is my prayer.

M. B. HADLEY."

CHAPTER XVII.

Effect of Mr. Hadley's death—Doubts and diffidence of the Board—General Conference action.

THIS was a dark day for Sherbro Mission. It was a time that tried the souls of the most earnest supporters of the cause of missions in the Church. Mr. Hadley's return and death seemed for the moment to have shocked the Church so that it stood still, and wonderingly and doubtingly asked, "What shall be done next? Must the African mission, after all, prove a failure?" It was a time of sadness, as well on account of the loss of our faithful missionary, as the future prospects of the mission itself.

For nine months before his return, as if he had a presentiment of his approaching end, Mr. Hadley had been calling loudly for help; but no help was sent. The committee tried to find men to send to his relief, but none were found. True, there were some who talked quite favorably, and one or two had actually been appointed, but for one cause or another they all failed.

Meantime complaints began to be made thick and fast that this mission was costing the Church entirely too great a sacrifice in life and treasure. One man had actually died! and the cry was renewed that Providence was against us. I hope the reader will not forget that up to this time, among all the persons employed by the Board to labor at Shengay, while all have suffered more or less from sickness, Mr. Hadley was the only one that had died. Instead of regarding his death, therefore, as a token of God's displeasure, the Church ought, and did finally, consider it as a mark of his favor and approval, that the lives and health of our missionaries, taken altogether, had been so precious in his sight.

But facts are stubborn things; only a few souls had been converted during all the years we had labored in Africa; the first chapel built had been devoured by the "bug-a-bug;" our faithful missionaries had returned, and one of them died, and there was nobody to take their places. The church, in many localities, was restless, and in some instances censorious. With this unsettled state of things the Board of Missions was itself inclined to waver. Happily their annual session, just after Mr. Hadley's death, was held at the same time the General Conference convened. The old Board held a session at Annville, Pennsylvania, just before the meeting of the General Conference at Lebanon, Pennsylvania. At this session the Board did little more than take a retrospective view of their work. The secretary and treasurer made their reports. Of the African mission the secretary said, sorrowfully:

"Though the prospect is not very flattering, I can not but believe that a glorious harvest of souls will yet be gathered among that people, and that before long, by that church that will sustain laborers there. The people among whom we labor there are very similar to those in Sierre Leone, where Johnson, and During, and others labored with such marked success about thirty years ago, many of whom and their descendants are respectable Christians. In a very few years our mission will be in this colony; and if we could 'hold fast the profession of our faith without wavering,' which is that the gospel is adapted to the wants of even the most degraded, we might yet see our efforts crowned with abundant success. Under the circumstances, however, I shall not oppose stoutly the abandonment of Africa; and for the reason that if it is continued the probability is that it will sustain such a meager support as to greatly protract its seeming failure."

After expressing the wish that the whole matter might be referred to the General Conference, and a willingness to abide by their decision, he dismissed the subject.

The Board were as doubtful as the secretary. Only one member was at all pronounced in favor of prosecuting the mission. Others would be glad to do so, but feared we could not. Still others thought we could accomplish so much more good with the same money elsewhere, that we ought to project a foreign mission in some other place. With these conflicting hopes and fears and expressions, the question was referred to the General Conference.

In a few days more the question, Shall the Sherbro Mission be continued? was brought before the General Conference. The Committee on Missions recommended the passage of the following:

"*Resolved*, That the Board of Missions make an arrangement with the officers of the American Missionary Association, or others, to take charge of our mission-station in Africa, until such time as the Board shall see its way open to prosecute the work properly."

Pending this question there arose a spirited debate which showed that while some were doubtful, others strongly opposed, there were many who zealously favored the prosecution of the work.

Dr. Davis said: "I hope the General Conference will not dispose of the African mission in any such summary way as this. I hope, if it is the sense of the General Conference and the Church to get rid of the African mission, that they will do it at once, so that we will know that that is the intention.

"I listened to the counsels of the Board, and it seemed to me that there was an intention to set that mission aside. It gave me pain. I do not think that our brethren in the West generally wish it. My own convictions are that if you are not able to sustain the mission there, you should simply let it rest in the hands of the Board until men and means can be found to prosecute the work."

These were timely words. Others followed in a similar train of remark. Finally Mr. Speck, of the Alleghany Conference, offered the following as a substitute for the committee's resolution:

"*Resolved*, That the African work be left in the hands of the missionary Board with discretionary power to supply it with men and means as soon as practicable."

The Conference now called on Mr. Flickinger for all the information which he possessed in regard to that mission. This he gave, and closed his remarks by saying the question had been brought here for the purpose of having the General Conference settle it without any bias from himself or anybody else. A number of members spoke, some for and some against the mission. At length Bishop Shuck said: "I would rather that the whole thing die and be buried as one of our missionaries has died and been buried, than that we should hand over to another party so important a part of our work. Other Christian organizations are planting their standard on foreign soil. We have had our sentinels out. One has been brought home to die; others have returned, and the pulsations of spiritual life which were beating in their hearts have become palsied because of the want of vital interest at the base of operations. If we deliberately hand over this work to another organization, is it not natural that the hearts of the people beating in sympathy with this cause will feel like join- that other division of the army and going on to glorious victory? When we pass the resolution of the committee, Ichobod will be justly written upon our banner in the missionary cause, and the very life-blood of our whole missionary operations will measurably cease to flow. *I* say, let this matter go with a way wide open to the Board. Let it say to the Church, 'The way is open,' and I believe the money and the men will come. It seems to me that the very death of that devoted missionary is the life of the foreign missionary enterprise in this Church. We have but too few who are willing to die in the cause. We can not, in our purposes at least, be true to our mission on earth and refer the work as the report proposes."

These burning and righteous words had a good effect. Mr. Speck's substitute was adopted by a large majority, and the Board advised to "keep the door wide open" for missionary labor in Africa. Being thus reassured the Board no longer hesitated. The question was settled. Through evil report and good, with bright prospects or dark, the Sherbro Mission must be kept alive. It would have been unwise, cowardly, and false to ourselves as a Church, and to the missionaries who had thus far labored in the field, to have thus summarily abandoned it. The reader will no doubt wonder that the Board, or any part of the Church, ever thought of vacating or delivering over to another party, which amounted to the same thing, so important a part of their work.

CHAPTER XVIII.

Appointment of Mr. and Mrs. Gomer—Meeting in Dayton—Departure—Arrival in Shengay.

THE door was now wide open; but who would enter it? One call after another was made, but none answered. The committee were anxious to send missionaries, but none could be found. They waited, and prayed, and hoped. Mrs. Hadley alone signified her willingness to return whenever the Board judged it proper for her to go. The Executive Committee sought for some minister who could take his wife and make his residence at the station, but it was difficult to find one.

Time passed. Another meeting of the Board was held. Here again the subject was thoroughly canvassed. It was finally agreed to commit it to the care of the Executive Committee, with instructions either to send missionaries, or if these could not be obtained, to form an alliance with the American Missionary Association, whereby they might supply it with laborers, we defraying the expenpenses, till we would furnish missionaries ourselves. But this proved impracticable. Finally Mr. Flickinger proposed to go again to Africa himself as a missionary; but the committee did not feel authorized to send away their secretary.

At length it was agreed to renew the proposition that had been talked of for a year or two, to send Mr. J. Gomer and his wife of Dayton, Ohio. Mr. Gomer was a colored man of superior intelligence and piety, and had often said if he was satisfied that he could be of service in leading his race to Jesus, he would be glad to go to Africa as a missionary. The committee were personally acquainted with him, and knew him to be one of the most thorough and wide-awake Sabbath-school superintendents in Dayton; and although he was not a minister of the gospel they believed he would make an effective missionary. They knew him, moreover, to be a thoroughly honest, industrious, faithful Christian gentleman. He had been employed for a number of years by a large business firm in Dayton, and enjoyed their utmost confidence.

When the question was asked, Will you go

to Africa? Mr. Gomer responded, "Yes," and his faithful wife answered, "Yes; we'll go gladly." The committee began to feel then, and the opinion has been gaining ground ever since, that in selecting laborers for Africa, they were like Samuel and Jesse choosing a king for Israel. All the seven sons were sought before David, the shepherd boy. So the committee were looking abroad, and probably to outward appearances, not duly considering that the Lord now, as in the days of Samuel and David, "seeth not as man seeth; for man looketh on the outward appearance, but the Lord looketh on the heart." However this may be, they seem to have been remarkably slow in sending this man of God to point his fellow-countrymen to the Lord Jesus. If he had been a preacher he would doubtless have been sent long before.

After the appointments were made, and Mr. and Mrs. Gomer were ready to start, a farewell meeting was held in the Third United Brethren church in Dayton. It was one of the most impressive gatherings, in many respects, that ever assembled in the city. Many citizens and members of other evangelical churches, as well as large numbers from the several United Brethern churches of the city, were present, not merely as idle spectators, but as hearty sympathizers in the work to which Mr. Gomer and his wife had consecrated themselves. They were there also as personal friends and brethren in the Lord, having come to bid them farewell, and personally to express their desires for their safe journey to Africa, and for their abundant success in the blessed work of saving souls.

Mr. Gomer's remarks on that occasion impressed all that if he were not ordained of man to the work of the ministry, he had a higher anointing for that holy office. He expressed such faith in the gospel for himself and for the heathen in Africa as to leave no doubt that he would do whatever man could perform to show the people the way of life. Mrs. Gomer also made remarks which showed that she was personally acquainted with the way of life, and as thoroughly alive to the dying condition of the heathen as her husband. Other members of the congregation with which they had been connected for years also made remarks. Several members of the committee spoke; and when the meeting closed there was but one opinion concerning it, and that was, that "God is in this place," and that he was there to signify to both the missionaries and the Board his approval of the work they had undertaken to do. It was remarked by an eminent divine of the city that he regarded it as a special mark of honor conferred upon the Third United Brethren Church, that God had passed by the splendid temples and wealthy congregations of Dayton, and selected from this humble church laborers for so important a work. But this is in keeping with his word; "for ye see your calling, brethren, how that not many wise men after the flesh, not many mighty, not many noble are called."

Bidding farewell to friends, and home, and native country they started on their long journey on the 8th of November, 1870. They were accompanied to New York by Mr. Flickinger. After a few days spent in preparation they took passage for Africa *via* Liverpool. This route, though farther and more costly, is much more easily and speedily traversed than by direct sailing from New York to Freetown. They landed in Freetown the 11th day of January, 1871, and in a few days, accompanied by Mr. Burton of the

Mendi Mission, they went to Shengay. Mr. Burton introduced them to the king, who received them with expressions of hearty congratulation. Mr. Gomer made him a small present. The king talked very friendly, and told him he might teach school and hold meetings in the barre, or court-house. In a few days after he held a meeting in the barre. The king was there and quite a number of the people. Mr. Gomer wrote:

"My wife and myself are both delighted with our new home; think we will like it very much. The house and everything about it is in a bad condition. The out houses all want repairing The king treats us very kindly. There was a miserable fellow in command here. I will make out a full statement of everything in my next"

It was very evident that the mission was no longer watched over by its faithful friend, Mr. Williams; and had the committee not sent laborers soon the mission property would have been utterly destroyed. But our missionaries took possession and went to work with a determination to do what they could in this new and strange field of labor.

They soon discovered that while the mission was deprived of the labors of men for a time, God had been working among the people. Perhaps Mr. Williams' death had made an impression on their minds which neither his life nor teaching could do. Possibly the being left alone to think on their ways, in contrast with the requirements of the gospel as they had been set forth by the missionaries, caused them to awake and consider. Or, perchance, they were more inclined to listen to the gospel from missionaries of their own color. But whatever the cause, the fact was apparent. The king and family and many of the people were inclined to listen to the gospel with more interest than ever before.

Mr. Gomer was greatly encouraged by these omens of interest and faith on the part of the people. He believed it to be the period for the success of this mission. In his opinion the salvation of that part of Ethiopia drew nigh, and he set himself to improve the rising tide. He held meetings regularly at the mission house; he reorganized the Sabbath-school, and being invited by the king, held frequent meetings in the barre, or courthouse of the town. These meetings were most always attended by the king and most of the members of his numerous family. The king was very old and feeble, and sometimes he was not able to walk, and he would have his servants carry him to the barre.

He did more. He enjoined it upon his slaves to attend the meetings. This was a long step in advance of anything he had ever yet done. Hitherto he had forbidden them to go to the meetings or schools of the missionaries. Let no one ask in astonishment, "Why did he not liberate his slaves?" His eyes were not yet opened. He only began to realize that he needed light. Moreover, he recommended and encouraged all the free people of the town to attend the meetings. The consequence was that from the very first Mr. Gomer had large congregations, and his words came to them in demonstration of the Spirit and of power. The people literally "thronged to hear him." His letters show that the interest which had so often been manifested on the part of a few was extending to persons of influence, and widening like a wave of the sea, awakening a spirit of anxious inquiry among the hundreds who had never before heard or understood or believed the gospel. They came also from neighboring towns to hear him preach, and he had frequent invitations to go to other villages to preach.

As these tidings were brought from time to time to the Executive Committee they were forcibly reminded of Mr. Gomer's remarks on the evening of his departure. "I believe," said he, "that there is power in the gospel to save the heathen; and I believe, God helping me, I can make *them* believe it too."

CHAPTER XIX.

Difficulty of holding converts—Children under the influence of heathen parents.

ONE of the greatest difficulties that confront our missionaries in Africa is the continual and wide-spread, in fact universal, bad example of the people at large. If a man is partially enlightened and convicted of sin, or even converted, he has no one among his fellow countrymen with whom to associate, only such as are fully under the influence of idolatry and superstition. With such associates, such bad example, and the continual reproach, scorn, hatred, spite, and mockery that he is compelled to face, it is no wonder that he begins to shudder, to hesitate, and, alas, that he too often goes back "like the sow that was washed to her wallowing in the mire." Often the missionary is first pleased when he sees some earnest listener to the truth come again and again to hear the word of life, and finally make a profession of faith in the Son of God; and then his soul is sunk in gloom as by his mind's eye he follows this same lamb of the fold out into the vast wilderness full of ravenous beasts, so foul, so cunning, so ready to deceive and destroy those who attempt to depart from the ways of sin. Many souls are thus lost. This indeed is no new thing, but is doubly discouraging in heathen countries. We have many wayside hearers of the gospel in this country, and are obliged to observe that the devil often "catcheth away that which was sown in their hearts." We observe also that many hear the gospel oftentimes repeated, and do not yield to its claims; and, oh, how frequently are we compelled to witness the sad defection of souls "who were once enlightened and had tasted the good word of God, and the powers of the world to come." But while we lose many here in this way, we also save many, and it does not seem so disheartening as where a minister in a heathen country has labored for years, perhaps, and then, after seeing a few souls yield to the truth be compelled to witness their reënslavement to Satan through the evil devices of the surrounding heathen.

This danger is greatly increased in the case of children. All know the impressible nature of children. All understand that it is from their ranks that Christianity wins its greatest triumphs. Our missionaries can have access to any number of children; but how save them? This is the question. They can teach them the truth, but they return to their parents to be taught falsehoods. Parents' words, all understand, go farther with children than any and all others. So these heathen children are frequently allowed to go to the day and Sabbath-schools of the missionaries in order to learn to read and write, but the truths of the gospel they are taught to reject and to cleave to the superstition of their parents. Thus it is that few children are at first, or can be at first, won to the Savior. Their parents stand in the door of the kingdom, assisted by the heathen priesthood, and neither enter the kingdom themselves nor allow their children to enter.

How to overcome this evil is one of the problems that the missionaries in all heathen countries have been obliged to grapple with. Some have held that the better way is to obtain control of as many children as a mission can support, and maintain them altogether in a separate condition from the heathen people surrounding them. But to this there are many and grave objections. It is very costly. Take fifty or a hundred children, and clothe them, shelter them, feed them, instruct them, and it will be found too heavy a drain on any missionary treasury. The support of a college in this country, where students pay for their clothing, lodging, boarding, books, and at least a part of their tuition, is an immense expense. How, then, could a mission be thus supported in a foreign land?

But is it best thus to cut them off at once and forever from their heathen ancestors and associates? Would they have as strong a hold upon them, and be as able to persuade them to become Christians as they would be had they remained among them, and retained an intimate acquaintance with their ways and wants? Moreover, would they not be more apt to relapse into idolatry than they would if they had been brought up in such conditions as to see it from day to day in all its manifold vices and soul-destroying delusions?

Whether such is the fact in all cases or not, it is manifestly impracticable, if not impossible, to isolate any considerable number of the heathen, either adults or children, from the mass of their fellow countrymen. The whole lump must be leavened. We must follow the apostolic plan. We must rely on the power of the gospel to convert their souls. Churches must be formed and thrown on their own resources with their own officers, teachers, and pastors, in the belief that God will cause the truth to flourish. Paul began in Corinth, Rome, and other heathen cities by simply and faithfully preaching the gospel. At first it seemed a hopeless task, but it did succeed, and so will the truth now. If some go back to the world, others will abide by the faith.

The following letter, written by Mr. Gomer shortly after his arrival in Africa, illustrates what odds young converts have to contend with. It also shows that in some instances God's grace in one man's heart proves itself to be stronger than the cunning of Satan in many hearts. The reader will understand that this is the Tom that Mr. Bilhiemer refers to as having been converted during his ministry at the mission. And from the conversation of this man with Mr. Gomer I think the reader will be ready to add him to the catalogue of souls saved by our missionaries at Shengay. What a multitude of sins may we not suppose have been hidden in Africa by the conversion of a few sinners from the error of their ways through the labors of our missionaries! But read the letter:

"SHENGAY, WEST AFRICA, March 14, 1871.

"The Murra Men are a tribe that are celebrated for their skill in making greegrees and charms. People here call it making medicine. There is one of the Murra Men here now. He told Tom that for four yards of cloth he would make him some medicine that would make his master like him past all the other hands. Tom said to him, 'God like me; and if my master no like me, your medicine no make him do it.' Another offered to make Tom some medicine that would make him a fine gentleman. Tom eyed the fellow as he stood before him half naked and dirty, and said, 'Why he no make *you* fine gentleman? You want to make me fine past you? I can't see how you do dat. I tink you want to make me fool one time.'

"I asked Tom one day if he had felt a change of heart at any time.

"'Please, sare, I can't tell; I tink so.'

"'Was it when Mr. Bilhiemer was here?'

"'No, sare, I bin try dis time, but I no catch.'

"'Did you pray?' I asked.

"'I been pray leetle, sare, but no too much; but when Mr. Bilhiemer be go, sare, I pray too much, sare.'

"'And then you were converted, you think, do you?'

"'I tink so, sare. Please, sare, I get cold.'

"'We are going to have prayer-meetings, and you must come and get warmed up.'

"'I come, sare.'

"When we were up to Harrowtown the people were having a grand powwow over some god of theirs. I asked Tom if he could get me a god. He went out and returned in a few moments, saying, 'Please, massa, I fetch him,'' handing me a smooth stone about the size of a large apple.

"'Where did you get him, Tom? said I.'

"'Please, sare, I tief him.'

"'But I don't think that's right, Tom.'

"'Please, sare, I don't think I can go to hell for dat.'

"Taking everything into consideration I

have hopes of Tom. They all want some one to oversee them. Tom is doing very well now. Yours in Christ.

J. Gomer."

CHAPTER XX.

Mr. Gomer's faithfulness—Visits Harrowtown—Day and Sabbath-school—Interest of the king in the mission.

MR. Gomer's labors in Africa have thus far been eminently successful. He goes to the people in such simplicity, earnestness, and faith that he immediately wins their confidence and impresses them with the importance of the message he brings. If he goes to villages on business, as he must frequently do, he takes occasion to preach to the people, visit the sick, and point all to Jesus Christ. That the reader may the better understand his mode of operations, the difficulties that lie in his path, and the prospect of overcoming them, I give below a part of a business letter written to the corresponding secretary the 11th of March, 1871:

"On the the 13th of February we reached Shengay, and on the 20th I opened a school in the barre in town with fifteen scholars. We were very much annoyed one day by loafers and bad children. They had a grand powwow all day near the barre, and the old man Caulker said they would frequently want the barre for court purposes, so I have moved the school out to the mission. We have twenty-seven scholars as the average attendance. Twenty-five scholars are in the third reader, two in the second, and the rest spelling in one syllable.

"Several of the children came to school naked. On the third day I cut off pieces of blue baft the proper length, cut a hole for the head, and at night told them they must take them home and have them sowed up, and then they might wear them while in school, but not out of school. Some of the boys never came back.

"I have had to be away considerable of late, and, not willing that the school should stop, I have employed Thomas Caulker to teach for me.

"My wife is also busily engaged. She teaches the little girls who come to school how to sew. She is also teaching the children to sing, and they are learning rapidly.

"Thomas Caulker professes to be religious. He is very anxious to teach school. He opens and closes the school with prayer. He has good order in school, and is a very good scholar himself. He also teaches a class in the Sabbath-school. I pay him 1s. 6d. per day. There was no one else here that I could get, and so far I like him well.

"I hold meetings on Sabbath. In town, I regret to say, the meetings are not well attended. A few come regularly, among them the whole of the Caulker family—the old man, George and his wife, Thomas, and James. George is not very regular. George and the old man profess to be very friendly, and say they are glad they have a colored missionary. The old man seems to be very much interested in the meetings. I believe that he wants to be a Christian.

"I go to their houses and talk to those who do not come to meeting. The excuse of some is that they have no clothes, others say they will come, but they never get there. Some stand outside the barre and look in. Mrs. Williams says they are not allowed to attend the meetings. Others say that it is not so, that all may attend who wish. I think that things will all come out right in the end.

"The Sabbath-school is about the same as

the day-school. Both ought to be much larger than they are. When I am at home I generally have a Bible class Wednesday nights, and as soon as possible I want to organize a prayer meeting. There are several here who profess to be Christians, and some say they want to be.

"On the first of March I went up the Cockbarrow River to Harrowtown. It is about thirty miles from Shengay. Satan has it all his own way there. The people say they never heard of the God of heaven nor of Jesus Christ. They say no missionary has ever been there before. Tom says Mr. Williams had been there, but never talked to them about God. I was there two days engaged in buying rice. I talked to some privately during the day, and at night I talked to them all at the barre. After talking about one half hour I stopped. 'Please, sah,' said Tom, 'dem say dey want you to tell um some more.' I then talked a while longer. They were very attentive, and desired that I should come again. Tom says that some of them told him that what I told them was true. One woman said next day that she had not slept all night for thinking of what had been said. She said she had always thought their was some other God besides theirs, but had never heard about him before. She promised that she would not worship their gods any more. I taught her to say, 'Lord, be merciful to me, a sinner.' She promised to say it every day till I came again. She is the head-man's wife, and I think she is sincere.

"I also talked to a girl about eighteen years of age who was sick. I told her of Jesus. Great tears rolled down her cheeks. She was too weak to talk. I should have liked to stop there longer. I would like to visit these towns often and talk to the people, but I can not well leave the school.

"I am very hopeful that good will be accomplished at Shengay. I had a long talk with old Mr. Caulker last night. He makes fair promises, if he will only keep them. He says Lucy Caulker, his daughter, was converted in this mission and is a Christian. He seems proud of her. God only knows the old man's heart. I leave all with God. Pray for Africa."

Several things in this letter appear wonderful. When Lucy Caulker was first converted*

---
*Chapter VI.

her parents took her away from the mission and severely punished her. Now she is greatly beloved of her father because she *is* a Christian! Then how strange to hear of Mr. Caulker and his whole family attending the meetings of our missionaries, and in every way possible helping to reach and save the people! Surely God is at work among these people. Mr. Gomer believes that the king wants to be a Christian, yet he scarcely dare say it lest somebody will call him fanatic or foolish. "But," says Mr. Gomer, "he acts and talks like a man who is heartily tired of sin. To me it appears he is sincere, but I can not read his heart. I leave the whole matter with God, who understands the whole case." On reading this one scarcely knows which to admire most, the king's change of conduct, or the missionary's humble trust in God.

CHAPTER XXI.

Conversion of King Caulker.

WE have seen what a great change has come over the headman of Shengay, Mr. Caulker. If the reader will go back to Chapter IV., when Mr. Flickinger visited him repeatedly in his exile at Bendoo, and observe how slow he was to grant the privilege to locate a mission in his territory, and remember his secret opposition to the mission for years after, he will be astonished at the bare suggestion of his conversion to God. If he will consider, moreover, that this man was brought up entirely under the influence and teaching of idolatry, and probably never heard of our Lord and Savior before he was forty or fifty years of age; that he owned many slaves, and had a number of wives, his astonishment will be greatly increased when he is told that this old man is converted. And yet such is the report—I was about to say the fact. And why not? Have we not known persons converted at an advanced age in this country? Have we not known great sinners to be forgiven? Is anything too hard for the Lord? But can a slave holder or polygamist inherit the kingdom of God? Certainly not as such. But can not God forgive such if they repent? Has he not promised to save to the *uttermost all* them that come to him by Jesus Christ? The only question, then, is, Did Mr. Caulker repent? Was he really penitent? To these questions we can only reply that he acted like he was very penitent. For three or four months before he died he was a changed man as to his entire conduct. He forsook the worship of idols. He sought for forgiveness through Jesus Christ. He professed faith in Christ. He prayed. He said God was good and precious to his soul. He attended public worship, and bore the cross himself before the people. He recommended Jesus Christ and his salvation to the people, urging them to commit their souls to him, and to give up their idolatry and superstition.

In a letter dated June 15th, 1871, Mr. Gomer writes:

"We are still very much encouraged in our work, and I think we have good reason to be.

Our meetings are all well attended. Often at the barre great numbers stand outside, for want of room inside. We have prayer and speaking meeting Sunday nights at the barre. The building is illuminated with palm oil light.

"Last Sabbath night I think nearly one half stood outside. Old Mr. Caulker himself spoke to the people and urged them to become Christians. He said that he prayed to God, and that God had blessed him, and he knew that religion was good. He spoke in the Sherbro language, and the people were very attentive."

On the 25th of June he again wrote: "I was quite feeble from fever, but started very early, took my time, and walked into town to the barre. I found the chief already there. He is usually the first one there, and tells the people they ought all to be there before the missionary comes. I got into a hammock and rested myself till 11 o'clock. By this time there was a very good congregation. The meeting was opened with singing and prayer. Mr. T. Caulker, Jr. read and interpreted the 95th Psalm. I then talked to the people for half an hour from the fourth verse of the 23d Psalm.

"At night Thos. Caulker conducted the meeting. After prayer the congregation sung:

> " 'Just as I am, without one plea,
> But that thy blood was shed for me,
> And that thou bidst me come to thee,
> O Lamb of God, I come.'

"The venerable chief then spoke to the people in the Sherbro language. He gave them a brief account of his former life. He had been a man of war, but God had been good to him. He knew that God had protected him, and he was thankful to God for his goodness to him. He knew that it was good to serve God. He hoped that everybody would serve God and become Christians. God had sent them a missionary of their own color to teach them how they ought to live. He hoped that God would bless Mr. Gomer and his wife and give them long life.

"On Friday a big palaver was brought to Shengay from a small town. A man had broken their law, and when they went to arrest him he ran off and hid. Then they seized his two wives and all his goods. He came to protect his wives and goods, and all were brought to the chief for trial. Saturday the case was not ended. Mr. Caulker told them they would hold no court on Sunday, for that was God's day. They held meeting on Sunday. One man said he would not live in such a town, he would go home."

Thus it will be seen that Mr. Gomer has good reason for believing that the chief is converted. He feels just as all Christians should feel, that it is a great triumph of grace, and another signal token of God's favor to the mission and of his approval of the work we have undertaken to do. True, Mr. Caulker's soul is worth no more than any other man's soul, yet his conversion at his advanced age, and the influence it will have in leading others to the cross, should call forth devout thanksgiving to the God and rock of our salvation.

But it will be still asked, Did he liberate his slaves? And what did he do with all his wives? He did just nothing at all. What he would have done if his life had been prolonged no one can tell. Nor can any one tell in his condition as a heathen how far he must go to be accepted of the Lord. God judges men according to what they have, and not according to what they have not. How much the Lord may have required of him, and how far he went in his desires and purposes, are questions we may not be able to answer. Still we are to believe that the Lord Jesus came to save men, not to destroy them. He has saved many others as old, as guilty, and as near to hell as Mr. Caulker. Why, then, may he not have saved this old chief? He thus gave an earnest of the salvation of the people as soon as they believe. Now that the old man has gone they will remember his words and his prayers just before his death, and be inclined to seek the salvation of their souls. At any rate we may safely rest his case in the Lord's hands.

CHAPTER XXII.

Other souls converted — Cheering prospect — More help wanted.

IN June Mr. Gomer wrote that the people were greatly interested in the schools and meetings of the mission. Every canoe that landed at Shengay sent a delegation to the mission "to tell them how d'ye." Said Mr. Gomer: "Men and women come with a headache, a colic, a sore foot, or a sick baby. The men get into palavers (disputes or quarrels), and come to me to adjust the difficulty. All must be waited on. Thomas interprets for me. He sings and prays and talks to the people very earnestly about religion."

He had at this time a wide door of usefulness opened to him. The people thronged to him, some for one purpose and some for another, but among the many there were no doubt some who came sincerely inquiring the way of life. Of his efforts Mr. Gomer wrote: "On Wednesday nights we have meetings in the mission parlor. Quite a number attend. Some nights the parlor is crowded. Quite a number speak and express a desire to become Christians. I think that several are in real earnest. Among them is one of George Caulker's wives, and one son about nineteen years of age, and one of old Mr. Caulker's daughters. Thomas, my headman, is doing splendidly. I can find no fault with him. He says God blesses his soul and makes him feel good in his heart. Two more of the mission hands have spoken in meeting and asked to be prayed for. In the Sabbath-school we have had as high as seventy scholars, but for the last two Sabbaths we have had but fifty-six scholars and seven teachers.

"I forgot to say, in the proper place, that I have organized two classes for seekers. I have one, and a Sierre Leone man that is stopping here has the other. Some of the seekers are too timid to speak in the public meetings, so we have private meetings. I think it a good plan.

"On Monday night my class met at the mission. The class is for professors and seekers. One old man who wants to serve God joined the class. He asked Mrs. Gomer what he must say when he got up.

"On Wednesday night I was able to attend the prayer-meeting. After several had spoken a poor cripple followed by the name of Farrbooto. He has been very attentive to all the meetings. He said: 'This gospel no come for Sherbro country people. The gospel be for white people, and people what sabba (understand) book.' He said he was a poor sinner and had nowhere to go. He wished God would have mercy on him. He liked for to go to heaven, but the gospel was not for such as him. He spoke in Sherbro. This is the interpretation.

"On the first Sabbath in July George Caulker volunteered to interpret for me. There was a chief present from the Turtle Islands. He has been stopping at Shengay several weeks. He spoke to the people about the new and strange things he heard from the missionary. He said he knew nothing of this God palaver before he came here, but he believed it was all true, and he was going to leave one of his boys here to learn about it in the mission school. This he has done."

These quotations will impress the reader

with the sad condition of these poor people. They are ignorant to the last degree. They are without hope, and without God in the world. They literally "sit in the region and shadow of death." It is very touching to note how sad they feel, and express themselves as being forsaken and uncared for by the great God. It is a deplorable state. And then the missionary has great difficulty to communicate with them even if they are ever so anxious to learn, and he ever so anxious to teach them. It is a tedious process. No wonder one said plaintively that she never knew anything of the great God, for nobody ever told her anything about him, and another that this gospel was only for white men or book men. These expressions so often uttered in conversation, leave no room to doubt that there is quite a wide-spread feeling among these people of guilt, of desolation, of wretchedness and woe, resulting from their ignorance of God and his Son Jesus Christ.

But the reader will observe an anxiety to find a better way. They seek the light. As the day dawns upon them they look up and thank God. When the missionary of the cross preaches to them they urge him to come and preach to them again. They hang upon his words with great interest. This is certainly a very hopeful feature. The Church should regard this as the the Lord's set time to favor Zion in Africa, and rally her forces. "Ethiopia is stretching forth her hands to God." The Church ought, therefore, to improve the rising tide. We have waited and worked long in the hope of saving souls in Africa, and now that the people are beginning to turn to the Lord every man should buckle on the armor and march to the front, for

> "There is a tide in the affairs of men,
> Which, taken at the flood, leads on to fortune;
> Omitted, all the voyage of their life,
> Is bound in shallows and in miseries,
> On such a full sea are we now afloat;
> And we must take the current when it serves,
> Or lose our ventures."

Mr. Gomer early observed this rising tide, and resolved to make the most of it. He and his wife went to work with great earnestness, doing whatsoever their hands found to do with their might. Nay more, he put others to work. Whoever could be found that might be induced to do something to instruct their fellows was immediately mustered into service. He hereby showed his capacity not only to comprehend the situation of things, but to take advantage of them, control them, and bring the people into subjection to his plans of operation, and ultimately to the truth itself.

He also began to communicate to the Board his need of reënforcements. He wanted more preachers, more teachers, more books, more of everything that would enable him to go on with the work. In one letter he writes: "I have visited several towns up the rivers. It is distressing to see what a strong hold the enemy has upon the people. We ought to have more laborers. Give us more help; but let it be of the right kind." In another he wrote: "I look for help this fall. Be sure and send some one to take charge of the finances. I am willing to do anything else. Please send a few common Bibles and some United Brethren hymn-books. I know you will pray for us in Africa." And in still another he said: "I urged Mrs. Hadley to come here. We need her very much. The school children like her, and she could so well instruct the women here. They need a woman to talk to them. You say nothing in your letter about a new chapel. We ought to have one. If the school gets much larger our parlor will be too small."

CHAPTER XXIII.

Death of the king—The field large and ripe.

THE conversion of Mr. Caulker, the king of Shengay, has been already referred to. The reader has also seen what kind of man he was before the mission was located there, and how for long years our missionaries were obliged to contend with his tacit and sometimes open opposition to their labors. It now becomes my duty to record his death. And if the reader still has any doubts of the genuineness of his conversion, the account of his last sickness and triumphant death will certainly remove these doubts.

On the 28th of August, 1871, Mr. Gomer wrote to the corresponding secretary:

"Thomas Stephen Caulker, our old chief, or king, is dead! He died on the fifteenth of this month, between six and seven o'clock in the evening. I had been with him all day. His faith in God was firm to the last. He sent for me early in the morning and asked me to hold meeting. I read passages of the scriptures, and several of us sang and prayed with him through the day. In this he took pleasure. He talked mostly in the Sherbro language. His pains were severe, but he bore them with patience. The last words that I heard him say in English were, "Salvation only through Jesus Christ; Jesus Christ is very merciful," and at the conclusion of a prayer in Sherbro he said, "For Jesus Christ's sake. Amen." He talked much in Sherbro. William and Thomas Caulker were both present They said he was sometimes talking about God, at other times he was praying. It was near six o'clock when I left the mission. I had just finished my dinner when I heard the cry. The whole town set up a howl or cry. Those who were present say he died quietly, and was sensible to the last. George was not in town, but came the next day. He made the people behave themselves, and sent for me. We had reading of Scriptures, singing, and praying at the wake.

"The town was full of strangers when the old man died, having heard that he was very sick. The funeral took place on the seventeenth, at Tasso, about three miles up the coast.

At George's request I went with them and held burial services. The Purrow Society were out in full force, and it was with difficulty that I was permitted to say the ceremony and pray. George interpreted the whole of it. The people here were too many for George. He could not manage them. He does not belong to the Purrow Society, neither did the old man. But the society took possession of the deceased chief, called up the devil, drank rum, and had a great time, lasting more than a week. The most of Shengay remained in Tasso several days, mourning and drinking rum. Such is heathenism. George came home and attended meeting on the Sabbath, and went back Monday. People are still coming in every day from all parts of the country.

"Some people will not believe that the old man Caulker has gone to heaven. They say he was too wicked. They do not believe God ever forgave his sins. They think he just fooled the people by saying he had religion. I can not say whether he is in heaven or not. I judge from the man's actions. Since the middle of last March there was a great change in the old man. He told me that God had blessed him, and when strangers were in town on Sundays he would always tell them they must attend meeting at the chapel. I believe I told you in a former letter about his speaking in prayer-meetings. There are many things that I have noticed which strengthens my faith in him, besides many prayers have been offered in his behalf at his request. Are these prayers all lost?

"George Caulker, who is now the king of the country, requests me to get everybody into the school that I possibly can. I hope the churches at home will pray earnestly for his conversion. Will you see that they do it? He has a great influence over the people that we need in the church. I believe God will give him to the church if the church asks for him.

"Our day-school of late averages about thirty, several of them slave children. All may attend now if they wish; and for this victory over Satan I thank God.

"You say nothing in your letter about sending a preacher out here. There are people here who want to be baptized, and others who desire to be married. A young man came to me a few days ago and got a piece of cloth to give to the mother of a young girl that he is going to marry, and requested me to marry them 'American fashion.' I told him that I could not marry him as I was not a minister. He seemed very much disappointed. I told him that I could send and get an English minister, and have him married English fashion and that would do just as well. He agreed to this, and we are to have an English wedding at the mission.

"The people here still insist on calling me a preacher. To please the people I preached a funeral sermon for old Mr. Caulker. I think that when God calls me to preach he will qualify me. I can talk and work among these country people very well, and they seem well pleased; and when they speak or pray they thank God for sending them a missionary of their own color."

Before Mr. Gomer went to Africa he had been repeatedly urged to accept license to preach the gospel, both by his own congregation and by several ministers, but he always refused, saying he thought he could do more good with his attainments and surroundings without it. Since he has gone to Africa, however, the quarterly conference to which he had belonged for years received a recommendation from the congregation and granted him license to preach. The document was forwarded to him, and was really on the way when the foregoing letter was written. So that he was soon not only called of the Lord, but duly commissioned of the Church to solemnize marriage and administer the ordinances of the house of God, as well as preach the everlasting gospel.

CHAPTER XXIV.

Farming—Commerce—Wages—Courtship—Marriage.

THE state of society existing in Africa, the deep degradation of the people, the pressing necessity for the gospel, and its civilizing, saving influences are forcibly illustrated by the following letter:

"REV. W. McKEE, Dayton, Ohio:

"*Dear Brother*—As you ask me to write something for the book you are preparing, I can not feel content without making an effort. You know that the different tribes have different habits and customs. What knowledge I have of the Africans relates chiefly to the Sherbro people. We are surrounded by the Gallians, Timmany, and Kossoos. There are many Mohammedans among these tribes. The Sherbroes are disposed to be rather an industrious and ingenious people, though their principal business is 'making farms,' as they call it. A farm consists of a half acre up to three, four, or six acres of land. Their principal crop is rice and cassada. They also raise large quantities of ground-nuts, yams, sweet potatoes, cocoes, corn and squashes.

"Fruit is not much cultivated as there is no market for it, and the natives seem to care very little for it. Plantains, pine-apples, bananas, mangoes, pears (not like the American pears) are cultivated to some extent. We have also the bread-fruit and the bread-nut that grows on trees. The cocoa-nut and a great variety of plums, and the guava out of which a delicious jelly is made, grow spontaneously. There are also many varieties of berries, growing wild, but these are chiefly sought after by the children.

"In making their farms they never cultivate the same piece of ground two years in succession, on account of the weeds, which they say 'grow too much.' No person owns any land individually. All belongs to the king, and each person can make a farm where he pleases. Last year we had four farms on the mission grounds, besides our own. They asked permission, however. By allowing them to make their farms we get the bushes cut down and cleaned away for nothing.

Farms are usually made just outside of the towns. No fence is made about them. In February the men with their cutlasses cut down the bushes which are very thick, gather up the vines and weeds, and when all are dry they burn them. Then the women plant the cassada, here and there, without any system. The seed of the cassada is the stalk. It is cut in pieces about four or six inches long. One end is put in the ground three fourths the length of it. It soon begins to grow. In a few days the men scatter the rice over the ground, and then dig the ground all over with a little implement that makes an effort to be a hoe. This done the women and children must keep the birds off till it is up pretty high. The men's work is now done until the rice is ready to cut. They can stay in town and amuse themselves by playing games, drumming, or visiting the other villages. Sometimes they fish and hunt. When the rice begins to head, the birds must be kept off again until it ripens and is cut. The birds are very troublesome.

"When they harvest the rice the men go into the patch with a knife or small stick with a sharp edge and clip off one head at a time.

It is tied in small bunches and hung on a stick or stump to dry. When dry it is tramped out by the feet or beaten out with a stick. After it is threshed it is put into very large baskets or 'bunkies,' as they call them. It is now ready for the trader.

"Many of the traders are colored men doing business for themselves. Many are agents for white men. Most of these men are natives of Freetown, Sierre Leone, and can read and write. They have been educated by missionaries, and their principal stock for trade is rum, tobacco, some miserably cheap dry goods, a few beads, earrings, charms, &c. The rice is soon exchanged for these articles, at an immense profit to the trader. The trader knows it is wrong to take advantage of these poor, ignorant creatures in this way, but their apology is that they are driven to it to procure for themselves a living. Having been educated by Europeans, they have adopted their dress and many of their customs. It costs something to keep this up. Freetown is thronged with applicants for situations. Clerks get from £1 10s. to £3 per month. Police-men get from £1 to £1 10s. per month. Mechanics get from thirty-six cents to $1 per day. Many have to support large families, and pay rent or taxes. They are frequently out of employment. Farming pays poorly. Large quantities of ginger and arrow-root are raised, but the prices paid by merchants are very low. They give what they please. As there is no market but Freetown they control the market. Palm-nuts are gathered in large quantities and shipped to England and France. Many ships and steamers go out of Freetown with full cargoes of palm-nuts, pea-nuts, ginger, and arrow-root. Hundreds of bushels of palm-nuts are never gathered at all. The hull of these nuts make a very good oil for cooking or burning. The nuts are boiled with this hull on. After boiling they are put into a mortar and the hull beat off. These are put into a large pot of water and boiled again. The oil comes to the top of the pot, and is skimmed off and boiled down. The nuts are then cracked by children, the kernel taken out and sold to river traders for rum at twenty-four cents per bottle, containing less than a quart. This miserable stuff is made in America, and very much adulterated here. The trader takes his kernels to town and sells them for cash.

"If the natives want fine oil, they put a quantity of these kernels in an iron pot, roast them thoroughly, then beat them and boil them as before. This is very tedious work, as the kernels require much beating. This is called nut-oil; the finest is called palm-oil.

"Wine is taken from the palm-tree by tapping it and holding a bottle to catch the sap. This the natives are very fond of drinking. In the very top of the palm-tree grows what is called the palm-cabbage, a very excellent vegetable.

"Each family has its house to live in, but it is not home. There is no family government. The wife is treated more like a servant than a wife, and the children raise themselves. If a man wants a wife he selects a girl, and takes a present to her parents, or owner, if she is a slave. This present is usually some sort of goods, blue or white baft, or satin stripe, or prints. Sometimes rum and tobacco is taken. If the parents are not satisfied with the first gifts, more must be taken; and when they are satisfied they let the girl go and live with the man. She now belongs to him. He can sell her or his children, or he can pawn them for money; and if he does not redeem them, the man who holds the pawn can sell them.

"One of the mission men had bargained for a girl, paid the goods required, and had a dress made for the girl to be married in, as he wished to be married 'American fashion.' When the parents learned this they refused to let the girl go. The father said that the 'white man fashion for marry was a bad fashion. People must swear, and that swear was a bad swear, for true, true.' His girl should not 'swear that swear.' She might go and live with him if she liked without swearing. But he refused to take her, as he professes to be a Christian, and wants to marry his wife.

"A man may have as many wives as he can get, and as a rule they live very pleasantly together. Parents have not the same love for their children here as in America. A chief that had attended meeting at the barre, sent a son to live in Shengay and be educated at the mission-school. Some wicked people told the boy that his father had sold him to the white man, (they call me white man,) and so he got in a canoe and went off up one of the rivers. Some weeks after the father happened at the town where he was, but would have nothing to do with him, saying 'he had no sense in his head.' He has sent another boy in his stead.

"Ever yours in Christ,
"JOSEPH GOMER."

CHAPTER XXV.

The New King—Catalogue of Converts.

AFTER the death of the old king, our missionaries were somewhat troubled about what might follow. George Caulker, the heir to the throne, was not a Christian. What if he should be a persecutor of the Christians? What if he should refuse to allow the missionaries to labor among his subjects? But these doubts and fears were soon removed. In a brief time the young king gave them assurances of sympathy, and every reasonable assistance that he could render. Thus they had renewed assurances that the King of kings is for them, and is opening a door for the gospel in Africa that no man can shut.

The following letter from Mr. Gomer, written a few weeks after the young king was enthroned, illustrates, incidentally, their fears in relation to the new sovereign. The letter is so fresh and life-like that I give it in full to the reader:

"SHENGAY West Africa, November 1, 1871.

"Rev. Mr. FLICKINGER, Dayton, O.

"*Dear Sir:*—I am happy to inform you that I am tolerably well to-day. I have had no fever for three days, but my wife is in rather poor health. The rains are about over, and the place is looking very finely.

"The porcupines and monkeys are beginning to trouble the cassada and ground-nuts. Tom caught one of the former the other day. Since the rains the snakes are very numerous. One of the boatmen cut a bunch of bananas, the other day, and he was bitten on the hand by a snake that was hidden among the fruit. A man who was present got some leaves and chewed them. He then sucked the wound and thus drew the poison out. This leaf is said, by the natives, to be the only thing that will cure the bite of this snake, and it must be applied immediately. A very large snake was in the top of the cane back of the house a few days ago. I sent to Shengay and got a gun to shoot it, but it would not make fire. Yesterday I went to visit a farm-house, and took one of the men along for a guide. The path was very narrow, and the bush was very high and thick. 'Walk fast, sir; walk fast,' said my guide. I looked up, and at my right, on a level with my head, was a green snake, five or six feet in length, crawling in the bush. Stephen, the guide, got a stick and dispatched him. I asked him if it was a bad snake. He replied, 'He bad for bite, sir; very bad; and he can't 'fraid for man.'

"Well, about the meetings. They have been neglected by me very much, of late. I have not attended night meetings in town at all for six weeks. I have held only one meeting in the day-time since I wrote you last. We were two weeks at Good Hope. The converts are all doing well, and I am happy to say that since I last wrote you three more profess to have found the Savior. One is one of the men's wives. Her husband also says he likes to pray and go to meeting, and that sometimes he can feel good when he prays. But he will not speak or pray in meeting,—says he is ashamed to speak. The third person that professes religion is the old woman, Na Yan Kin, who used to make mats on Sunday. For a long time she would not attend meeting because she had only one eye. She attends very regularly now,—says she has been praying for more than a month; that God has blessed her, and she is very happy; that she can never work any more on Sunday. I think these three are sincere. I observe them very closely as I have opportunity.

"I tell all the people that polygamy is wrong, and slavery, also; and I am doing all I can to put a stop to both. I am quite sure that the condition of the slaves is much better than when I came here. I am trying to have them all liberated, but I have to go slow.

"The Sabbath and day schools are both much smaller than they were before the old chief's death. I heard that George would not allow the slaves to attend; so I went to see him about it. He says it is false; that all who wish may go. But the rice is ripe now, and men, women, and children are kept busy driving the birds away. George is proud and despotic. This very morning he had his step-mother's brother—a married man—tied to a tree in front of his house and whipped very severely for a trifling offense. However he is very kind to the mission, and sends many presents of fresh meat since the death of the old man. He often kills a beef or goat.

"One of my men was tied and taken off the other night. He was the best hand I had, to work. He was sleeping in Shengay. He was a slave, and had run off four years ago.

"*Monday morning, November 6th.* This morning the man who had been carried away is at the mission again. He got away from his captors, though they had him tied hand and foot. His master lives about fifteen miles from this place. The slave is worth about six pieces of cloth, and wants me to buy him so he can work and redeem himself.

"I attended the meeting in town yesterday morning and evening. At night there was a large attendance, many having come in from their farms. George interpreted for me all day. At the close of the evening meeting he wished to read a text to the people. He read, with a few remarks, Proverbs xvi. 15 and xix. 12. The slaves all seem to have a sort of dread of him. He may be trying to deceive me.

"Perhaps you would like to have a list of those who have made a public profession of religion here. They are, the old Chief Caulker; Kate and Polly, his daughters; Jane and Jenny, wives of George; Kong, a slave; Na Yan Kin, a slave; Thomas and Stephen, mission hands; Farrbooto, the little man who said, 'The gospel not come for poor Sherbro people;' and Balla, the boatman's wife. I had a talk with the boatman's wife this morning, and she says she is sure her husband has been blessed. She says she tells him to talk in meeting, but he will not. I do not know these peoples' hearts. They tell me that God has blessed them, and I can not say he has not.

"*Freetown, November* 18*th*. I reached here on the 15th. I thought to find a letter here telling me when to look for Mrs. Hadley; but there was no letter here. I see in the *Telescope* that she is on the way. I see, also, that we are to have a preacher. I am very glad of this, for our cook is wanting to marry, and we need a preacher very much, anyhow. I see, also, that the Ludlow Street brethren have nicely complimented me by giving me license to preach. I am praying now that God will give me wisdom and make me a preacher, indeed.

"I am glad we are to have a nice boat.

God will reward those Sandusky brethren. They shall have my prayers. Will you pray for us? and for George Caulker especially? His proud heart must be humbled. God can and will do it, I believe.

"Joseph Gomer."

CHAPTER XXVI.

Two more missionaries sent—Letters from Mrs. Hadley, and Mr. Gomer.

AS the work increased in Africa the Board determined to send additional laborers. Mr. and Mrs. Gomer were doing well, but if one was sick it required the attention of the other. And there was more work than they could perfom. So the question was again asked, Whom shall we send to Africa? The answer soon came. Mrs. Hadley expressed her desire to return and work awhile longer for Africa; but the Board wanted a preacher. Mr. Gomer was not ordained; in fact he was not even licensed to preach the gospel when he went. A number of souls had been converted, yet it seemed improper for him to administer the ordinances of baptism and the Lord's supper, or to solemnize the marriage rite. He therefore insisted that the Board send an ordained minister to his assistance. Accordingly the Board appointed the Rev. J. A. Evans, of Grand Rapids, Michigan. He is a young man of fine ability, and fair education He was a member of the Michigan conference. After his appointment as a missionary to Africa he was ordained by Bishop Edwards at the annual session of the Michigan Conference, held in September, 1871, and about the last of October, of the same year, Mr. Flickinger accompanied the two to New York, and saw them sail for Africa. After a tedious and rather dangerous voyage, owing to stormy weather, they arrived safely in Freetown about the middle of December. Soon they were taken down the coast to Shengay, and immediately proceeded to the work they had gone to perform. I give below a letter from Mrs. Hadley shortly after their arrival:

"SHENGAY STATION, W. C. A., Dec. 19, 1871.

"BROTHER FLICKINGER: — Through the strange leadings of Providence I am again on the verdant shores of Africa, and in good health. I am truly thankful to God for permitting me to see with my own eyes the wonderful change which he has wrought among this people since my return to America. And I think no one can gainsay what has been wrought by our devoted missionaries, Brother and Sister Gomer. They have been pushing the battle to the enemy's gate, and I hope that many will be savingly enlisted under the blood-stained banner of King Emmanuel.

"The Sabbath-school and all the meetings are very interesting, and so is the day-school, in which the children have made good advancement. The speaking and prayer meetings are very encouraging, and I am encouraged to hear some bear witness that the seed of other years' planting had not been entirely lost, but, by the help of God, they prayed until he pardoned their sins. And never were there as marked omens of good as I now find among this people.

"Bro. Gomer is a real, live missionary. He goes to Shengay and talks to the people, and also visits them on their farms. He has even exposed his health in the rains, and, since we came, was sick with the fever. His wife is now having the chills, which I hope will be broken up to-day. I am really glad, for their sakes and the work's sake, that we are here to render them help and comfort. They have not only attended to the spiritual wants of the people, but the mission-house and its surroundings exhibit what they have done. The kitchen is good and convenient, and the mission-yard is well kept and improved. Bro. Gomer has also built a nice tomb over my child's grave, and placed the stones upon it in a good and substantial manner.

"Bro. Gomer has done much of his work among the people, in the way of teaching, by the aid of an interpreter, and he has succeeded in the work beyond all expectation. There is, surely, a great change taking place among this people. Even the young ruler is very favorably impressed, and renders most valuable service in our mission-work. He wields a great influence and power over the people to bring them under religious teaching. And we have bright hopes that he will soon be led into this great work, like Paul. He is a man of fine talent and education, and can turn the Scriptures into the Sherbro language in a ready and fluent manner. With what I know of the Sherbro tongue, and the thoughts that I can catch, he expounds the Scriptures well. Oh, may the Lord bless and save him! is the daily prayer of those so anxious for him here.

"For want of room in the mission-house

and the need of some special house of worship, on account of a large Sabbath-school and other meetings, it is necessary that we have a chapel built just as soon as it can be reared. And as we, in connection with the ruler and his people, think it best to have it in Shengay, we may build a school-house near mid-way to Shengay, that is, in the country style. The stone chapel you ordered built will be needed, also, as soon as it can be erected. Hurry up the money for it, as the one we are building will last but a few years, and both are needed,—the one in Shengay and the other nearer the mission residence.

"The ruler and his people are ready to render their help in this work, and, by the blessing of God, the house will be built. The rainy season has not yet closed, but I think we will not be troubled with much more rain. The weather has been quite cool, and we had a few very rainy days. Now you will please excuse us for any haste in our work, as our wants and the shortness of the dry season, with slowness in work here, demand us to move forward at once. And the people, also, are so favorable to this work now. You may think that it is not good for the missionaries to have the chapel so far away, and it will be more inconvenient in some respects; but in the end we will be able to secure the coöperation of the people in the work and in attendance; so we must work to gain the people and not so much to accommodate ourselves. We can get into our boat or be taken to Shengay in a chair or hammock when too feeble to walk, until the stone chapel is erected. Mr. Caulker says that if the house is there he can more strongly insist upon the people attending service. And you know this is so. And, again, it will give the town of Shengay another aspect. The people who visit Shengay will see it no longer the place for devil-worship, but the place for the worship of God. Already the word of this good work is spreading through the towns and country, and the change is observed in the people here by prominent persons in Freetown. Bro. Gomer has scattered much religious truth broad-cast, and much of the seed is taking root in good ground, that is in honest seeking hearts. God is moving the hearts of some in the mission-house; and I think Thomas Tucker, our head-man, is now a true Christian. He told me the other day that when all the missionaries were gone and he was left alone in the mission-house that the people here asked him, 'What you stop here for?' and he told them that this was the mission-house, and may be God would have some work for him to do; and, when Mr. Gomer came, that he began to pray again, for his heart got cold, and now he feels to trust in God. My heart has been filled with joy and gladness while hearing those new converts pray and speak, some in the Sherbro and some in the English tongue. May we still see sinners flocking home to God.

"I hope that a trip to Freetown and a change of diet will restore Brother and Sister Gomer to wonted health. We will try to take charge of the meetings and mission affairs in their absence. Thomas Caulker will teach the school and stop with us in the mission until the boat returns from Freetown. We will all be glad to get those supplies. I hope we will be able to do much good here. Pray for us.

"M. B. HADLEY."

I also furnish a letter from Mr. Gomer, expressing the gratitude of his heart and the prospects of the mission on the arrival of the new missionaries. The letter explains itself:

"SHENGAY, December 15, 1871.

"REV. D. K. FLICKINGER: *My Dear Brother:*—A great load has been removed, and now my heart is light. On December 9th, very late at night, a small boat landed at Shengay, with three passengers, namely, Mrs. M. B. Hadley, Rev. J. A. Evans, and Miss P. Williams. Mrs. Hadley engaged Princess in Freetown for company. They were in town several days before they got passage for Shengay. I received no letter informing me when to look for them. Mr. Elliott and the church missionaries I believe were very kind to them, and saw that they were well cared for. On the 10th we all attended meeting at the barra. As Bro. Evans wished to see just how I conducted the services, I delivered the morning discourse—the first after the receipt of my license. The young chief, Mr. George Caulker was present and interpreted for me, as Thomas was out of town. At the close of my sermon I introduced the two new missionaries. Each made a few remarks, the people giving the very best attention. Mrs. Hadley, in a very neat little speech, presented the young chief with a nice Bible and hymn-book—both sent to him by some well-wisher in America. Mr. Caulker was taken by surprise. He replied to Mrs. Hadley in a short speech, the substance of which was that he desired to be a good Christian; he sympathized with the work; a hypocrite was the most detestable of all persons; he cannot serve God and mammon; no one can say that he does not pray, for he does, and reads the Bible, and has read it a great deal; if he does not get to heaven it will be his own fault; he is very thankful to the Sabbath-school which sent these nice presents. Mrs. Hadley had other presents for Mr. Caulker; also, one book for Mrs. Caulker, which were given to them privately. At Sabbath-school we had fifty scholars. I did not go to the night meeting. Bro. Evans went; Mrs. Gomer and Mrs. Hadley also. Bro. Evans preached from Mark i. 1. The congregation was small, the night being dark and stormy. The next morning Mr. Caulker had all the people called to the barra. He told them that the law his father made would be enforced if they did not attend meeting; that their houses would not be protected, but any one who chose might plunder them.

"*Monday morning*, 18*th*.—Yesterday the meetings and Sunday-school were all well attended. There were sixty-five scholars at Sunday-school. We have determined to build a country chapel in Shengay. The people desire it there, and we thought it best to please them. Mr. Caulker has promised to help us; and all of his family are so well pleased with the prospect of their people becoming civilized and Christianized that they are willing to help. They are delighted with Mrs. Hadley, and the children think there is no one like her. They say, 'Dat missus good to me.' I think Satan's temper must be somewhat ruffled, for he has tried in many ways to weaken our hands and to hinder our work; but as we have a great work to do, we have given him to understand that the Lord's work can not cease. We have no time for palavers. We have prayed the prayer of Nehemiah, 'Now therefore, O, God, strengthen our hands.' Our plans for operation are not yet perfected. For the present Bro. Evans and myself are to preach alternately. Sister Hadley will assist Thomas Caulker in the school, for we think best to retain him there. Mrs. Hadley will also have charge of the sewing-class. Bro. Evans has charge of the books. Mrs. Gomer will look after the domestic affairs, while I shall have charge of the laborers. We all expect to take an active part in doing missionary work.

["And now there is a great cry among the laborers in the yard! A leopard came just to the edge of the mission-yard, and captured a chicken. The men try to catch him, but he makes his escape.]

"We have thought best not to organize a church class just at present, for certain reasons; but Bro. Evans will baptize several soon. On last Wednesday night, at prayer-meeting, three young men and two women arose and asked for the prayers of the Christians. Since then one of the men told me that he did not sleep all night, and felt very bad; but he prayed to God to have mercy on him. Now (Saturday) he begins to feel 'a little good.' He believes God will bless him. The Lord is with us, and the victory is ours. At present there is not a cloud to be seen. God is daily answering the prayers of his children. Tell our people to pray on. It is a good thing to give thanks unto God. We are wishing for an instrument for our Sunday-school. If any of the friends of the mission wish to present us with one, you may accept it.

"We shall begin at once to build a school-house on the mission-grounds, near the mission; also a chapel in Shengay. They are indispensable. We shall have to furnish lumber for doors, windows, and seats; also, a platform for Mrs. Hadley, as it will not do for her to be too much on the damp ground. She will be in the school most of the time. We shall have to have carpenters also, as we wish to hurry the work through while the dry season lasts.

"Keeping the mission-grounds in a proper condition has a good effect on some of the natives. Some of them say: "You got sense like white men." I tell them that when they worship the same God I do, and learn to study God's book and do all he tells them, God will give them sense like me.

"The converts are still doing well, and more are on the way. Mrs. Hadley is an excellent worker. She will do much good here; but she is working too hard; she will 'make herself sick.

"My wife and I will stay in town until the

goods and boat come. I do not think we ought to take a sea-voyage until after the school-house and chapel are built; and as soon as possible I wish to visit a few towns and test the enemy's works. I have promised to visit them. Mrs. Hadley wishes to go out also, and tell the people about Jesus. Every day people are dying who never heard of the Savior. Time is precious.

"I think your missionaries will get along nicely together. We will try try to keep the Lord in our midst to make the pathway smooth.

"Ever yours in Christ,
"JOSEPH GOMER."

CHAPTER XXVII.

D. F. Wilberforce.

When Mr. Flickinger was in Africa as a missionary he made the acquaintance of a very devoted native by the name of Wilberforce. He was employed at Good Hope station, on Sherbro island, while Mr. Flickinger was preaching for the American Missionary Association at that place. Mr. Wilberforce and his wife, though they had been brought up in entire ignorance of the gospel, were very faithful servants, and gave earnest heed to the things which they heard concerning their souls. About this time a son was born to them, and was named Daniel Flickinger Wilberforce, as a mark of respect for the minister who had but recently came to preach Jesus to them. As this soul's history is of considerable interest to all the friends of missions, I give room for an account of the way he came to be here, taken from an editorial in the *Religious Telescope*, September 11, 1872:

"When the child had grown to be a sprightly lad of about fifteen years of age, he accompanied a sick missionary of the Mendi Mission to America as a waiter, and after his arrival in New York was employed in the mission-rooms of the association for some time as an errand boy, in which capacity he proved not only very orderly and trusty, but extraordinarily expert. Last fall when the missionary secretary, Mr. Flickinger, was in New York making arrangements for our missionaries, Mr. Evans and Mrs. Hadley, to sail for Africa, he one day felt impressed with the duty of saying a few religious words to this orderly but active colored boy, whose good offices had for some days attracted his attention, but whose name, parentage, and native land were to the secretary entirely unknown and unsuspected. He introduced his homily by asking the boy his name. The reader may judge of Mr. Flickinger's surprise when they are told that the youth quickly responded, *Daniel Flickinger Wilberforce*. This led to inquiries and answers which developed the fact that this was the same child born at Good Hope, Africa, when Mr. Flickinger was there but of whose birth and name

Mr. Flickinger had become almost oblivious.

"The youth expressing an ardent desire to obtain an education, and having already made considerable progress in the elementary branches, Mr. Flickinger, after earnest prayer and thought, and counsel with the officers of the American Association, proposed to the Executive Committee of our missionary Board to take the youth in care on trial for the purpose of educating him in hope of his becoming a Christian teacher, and perhaps a preacher in his native country, and in his mother tongue, for he well understands the Sherbro language, which is that used among the people where our African mission is located. The suggestion was adopted, and the youth came to Dayton, and was placed in a pious, intelligent family, members of our colored church here, and sent to the colored school, where his good deportment, devotion to study, and good progress elicited the highest praise from Mr. Solomon Day, the accomplished teacher of the colored public school. He is orderly, modest, polite, intelligent, and cleanly, and has a high place in the affections and esteem of the family in which he lives, the members of the colored church where he is a regular worshiper, and of our prominent brethren in this part of the city.

"Last winter, at a revival meeting held by Rev. J. Nicholas, pastor of the Third United Brethren Church, one evening when the editor was present, young Wilberforce was soundly converted to God at the altar of prayer, and the next evening we had the pleasure of receiving him into the Church. Since that time his life and devotions have been such as become the religion of the world's Redeemer. Few American youths excel the pattern set by this native African; and we have just reason to hope that he will prove very useful somewhere, and probably in his native land, to which he proposes returning as soon as he has attained to age and culture sufficient to labor efficiently there.

"We hope the whole Church will pray that he may be kept by the power of God unto salvation, and that he may become a mighty instrumentality for the elevation and salvation of his race. Born in Africa, well versed in the Sherbro language, and possessing good mental endowments, he gives just occasion to hope that God intends him to do very valuable missionary work for the Church into whose care and communion he is providentially thrown. By race identified with his countrymen, (being a full-blood African,) having spent his youth among them, thus becoming completely identified in patriotic feelings with his native land, and being acclimated both by race and residence to the malaria of the western coast, it does seem that this youth, now about sixteen years of age, is peculiarly promising as a candidate for the African mission."

I am happy to add that this young man is now (November, 1873,) in attendance at Union Biblical Seminary, and bids fair to fulfill the highest expectations of the Board of Missions, and of the Church.

CHAPTER XXVIII.

Interesting letters — War palaver — Mr. Gomer as a diplomat.

By way of illustrating the habits and wants of the people in Africa, as well as the difficulties missionaries have to encounter, I give the following very interesting fragments of letters written by Mr. Gomer:

"SHENGAY, July 15, 1872.

"REV. W. MCKEE,

"*Dear Brother*—Our hearts have been made very sorrowful. One of our young converts has been taken from us. About two months ago she professed religion. It seems that when quite young she was betrothed to Chief Piomi, who is now between fifty and sixty years of age, while she is only sixteen. He came for her a few days ago, and went away yesterday, taking her with him to his home on the Turtle islands. She was unwilling to go, but was obliged to submit. I think her mother insisted on her going, for she is a very bad woman. It was she who had our sheep killed. The girl came out to the mission to bid us good-bye, and was feeling very badly. She has about one quarter white blood, and is a good girl.

"The people are fast learning how to keep Sunday here and in the villages. In one town on the Nambo there are two book-men who tell the people when Sunday comes. In some towns they make marks on the side of the house. At Mocaba a man makes marks on a piece of paper thus ||. Early on the morning of the seventh, he puts this paper on a long strip of board, hoists it up, and goes through the village, shouting at the top of his voice, 'Sunday dun come; no pusson kin work to-day.' I think it was in a village up the Walpalla that they lost their reckoning, and observed Monday instead of Sunday!

"A man came to the mission a few days ago to get a piece of cloth, to carry on a palaver. 'Ah! master,' says he, 'that palaver do me bad.' I say, Which palaver? 'Daddy, nah Picher die in my hand. I take um; go one town, he got sick; die. Nah, mammy say I must pay two-ten,'—about £10 in goods or slaves. 'I gie um four pieces cloth, two gallons of rum, and one ram goat. He no satisfy. Mr. Caulker he no talk um; mam mammy no more talk um. I go fetch next day, one gallon rum; make um feel good; he go throw cold water on um.' The man has two wives. One had a child about six years old. He took the child with him to another town, and it sickened and died. The grandmother made palaver with him, and said he should pay two-ten for the child. Mr. Caulker would not listen to the palaver. The man had already given the articles mentioned. To-morrow he would get one gallon of rum, and make the old woman drunk, and she would throw cold water on the palaver, and kill it.

"There were two conversions while I was in Freetown. And so the work goes on.

"*July* 25, 1872. We have been having a strong scent of war since I wrote last. On the 6th of this month George Caulker, our chief, left here for Bendo Toombah, to meet his chiefs, to settle a war palaver. A messenger met him there, from Bannah Bandah, chief of the Cockburrow tribe. The messenger had a cutlass, wrapped with a piece of white baft (bleached muslin), and a lock of a man's hair, and bore this message: 'Bannah says Mr. Caulker must pay two hundred slaves, or two hundred tuns of money (any kind of goods is money); if not, he must send the white baft back, with blood on it.' Mr. Caulker refused to do either until they talked the palaver, and the people refused to talk it. A man by the name of Boney, on the Tucker River, had a palaver. One Farmer Kendy, took Boney's part. One Carry Baw, interfered, and told his men to tie Kendy. They chased Kendy into the river and he was drowned. This is one story. There are many others. Boney's friends want to kill Carry Baw. He comes to Mr. Caulker for protection. The people demand him, but Mr. Caulker will not give him up without a trial. He gives Mr. Caulker the slip, and goes to the Kossoh country. Mr. Caulker has now come to MoCaba. When the people learn that Carry Baw has run off, they blame Mr. Caulker for it. They make Mr. Caulker a prisoner, and say they will not let him go until he brings Carry Baw. They began, now, to plunder the villages, to carry off the people's property, and to destroy things generally. They even tore the roof off the house where Mr. Caulker was staying, and let it rain on him. They send his servants away, and destroy the new rice which the people have planted, which is only a few inches high. Neither money nor slaves will satisfy them now. They must have Carry. Many reports are daily brought to us from the seat of war, from Bannah Bandah. We do not know what to believe.

"A canoe that landed here from one of the rivers reports that the mangroves are full of people, hiding from the war. In all of this, Mr. Caulker would not let his people fight, telling them that they must not shed blood.

"On the 12th of July, Shengay was all alive with excitement. Reports came that the Sierra Leone traders were sending their goods to British Sherbro. On the 14th, Sabbath, at meeting, we set apart Monday, the 15th, for fasting and prayer, after first speaking to the people from Joel ii. 12, 13. Monday the pews was very dark. There was a report that the enemy was coming to plunder Ben-Joo Toombah, near Shengay. The people of Shengay were sending their valuables, in boxes, to the mission, to be locked up in the basement of the mission-house. One good sister sent her child, five years old, to us for safe keeping. People were constantly asking me what I was going to do, and where I was going. The carpenter was annoying me all day about some provision for getting away from Shengay. He tried to hire our fisherman to go to Kent in his paddle-canoe, to hire a boat to come and take him away; and when the fisherman would not go, to throw away his life in the sea, the poor man cried like a child, and said that the savages would murder us all together, both English and Americans, and that he would never see his wife and children again. A canoe, with several persons in it, passing here to-day, flying from the war, was upset, but no one was lost. None of the missionaries have felt like leaving.

"On the 16th, at 9 A. M., I left my wife and Sister Hadley at the mission, believing that God would take care of them, and started in our little boat for Genda Mah, on the Cockburrow River, to Bannah Bandah, to see the war chief, and have a talk with him myself, I had seen this old man before, and talked with him about religion. I did not believe all the reports they brought about him. At 4:00 p. m. we reached Genda Mah; but the chief was at Matty Con, twenty-five or thirty miles farther up the river. We put up for the night at Mo Caba. (I have spoken of this town and the head-man before. His wife is the old chief's sister.) At night we had a meeting, and I think the whole town was present. I spoke, and Tom, my boat-captain, followed. The people remained after we dismissed them, and said they were very glad we were come. They said they would like to have us preach there all the time. They say they have kept Sunday ever since we were there last April. I asked if there was a 'book-man' there. They said 'No; but one man got good head. He make mark on the side of his house, and tell um when Sunday come.' They showed me the man. He was a fine-looking man, with a large country cloth thrown over his shoulder and wrapped about his body. At 6:00 next morning we were on our way up the river. At 10:00 we were at Matty Con. The old chief was in bed, hearing a canoe palaver. He has been for many years a leper, and the disease is now assuming a very bad form. His right leg, from his knee down, is covered with raw sores. He is to all appearance a man of good sense, for a native. His dress consists of several yards of India-blue baft, sewed together, thrown over the left shoulder and wrapped about his body. A black net cap, very much worn here, is on his head. He also has a pair of coarse shoes, which I have never seen him wear; but a boy usually carries them before him. He has a long cane with which he walks. His wives have all left him since he has got this disease. Leprosy is a very common disease here. It assumes many different forms. The old chief was very glad to see me, and denied knowing anything about the way the people were doing. He started a messenger immediately to the war party, and to Mr. Caulker, telling them that his people were acting contrary to his orders, and that they must return to him. The old man was very busy all day; so I could not get to talk with him much. At night we held a meeting. The attendance was good. I do not think, however, that the people were very well pleased with my discourse, for, while I was speaking, some of them went away. Others paid good attention. After we dismissed the meeting, a woman asked Tom if she must not 'keep stone for take care of her;' and if she must not 'cook for them (the idols), and give them palm oil for eat.' Tom told her, No; that it was all wrong. Bannah Bandah himself wears no charms nor medicines of any kind; says they are foolish things, and can do no good. The old man is well liked by all who know him. I believe that he would become a Christian if he had some one to teach him. He wished to know if we could not build a meeting-house at Genda Mah, and hold meetings there.

"Next morning (July 18th) Bannah Bandah asked me to write for him a letter to Mr. Caulker. I send you a copy, verbatum. I forgot to state that when I arrived, after telling him what I came for, he said: 'God bless you,—you a good man. My heart warm for you. Dat bad lie dem pusson can tell on me.' Turning to the people he said: 'You see pusson what got head. He can't hold um (believe um). Pusson what got no head,—ah! he can hold um. I sick and can't go no place; pusson can take my name and go spoil um all over the country.' And much more of the same sort.

"At 9:00 A. M., the 19th, 1 started for the mission again. The chief sent another messenger with me, with word to Mr. Caulker and the war people,—and Mr. Caulker has several under chiefs, Bannah Bandah being one of them. I reached home the same night, and found all well.

"The next day the people in Shengay thanked me very much for 'that walker that I do walk.' The people had changed their conduct toward Mr. Caulker. He was again at liberty to go where he pleased. One man that came from Mr. Caulker said that when the people heard that the 'white man' had gone to Bannah Bandah, 'they all got coward,' and many of them ran away home. All they want is to plunder, rob, and steal. I can not say what the end will be. They claim now that they have another message from Bannah Bandah, and that he says Mr. Caulker must buy the palaver.

"Mr. Caulker reached home on the 26th of July, and on the 30th started for Matty Con, to see the old chief."

Here is the letter referred to above:

Matty Con, July 18, 1872.

Mr. George Caulker, Chief of the Sherbro Country, western coast of Africa:

God bless you. When I see Mr. Gomer here, good how de do. Hush for the trouble what meet you there. I take you like my own heart. All what has happened there, I know nothing about it. Persons came to me from Boney four times, to show me this palaver. I took a cutlass and a piece of white baft, and a lock of the man's hair, and sent them to you, telling them that you must judge this palaver. They not do after the fashion I tell them. They should have judged the palaver after the country fashion. Why you no take some pusson and send to me for the truth of the matter? I sit down here; I hear that Carry Baw kill some pusson; that he run away; he pass here; I not know it. He has now got to the Kossoh people, I hear, to bring war on me for trying to kill him. When I hear that news about the way them people do to you, I can't hold it. So when I see Mr. Gomer I must hold it. So I write you these few lines. You must call all those head-men on that side and tell them what this letter says. With much respect, I am, very truly, yours.

BANNAH BANDAH.

These extracts show that our missionaries are exerting an excellent influence among the different rude tribes. Mr. Gomer makes a first-class diplomatist. His sincerity, tact, politeness, and good, common sense,—a quality often wanting in professional diplomats,—combine to render him influential in settling disputes, and preventing the recurrence of a clash of arms.

In due time the war clouds referred to passed away, and our missionaries found themselves surrounded by new and influential friends to help on the work.

CHAPTER XXIX.

Building a new chapel—Rev. Peter Warner and wife go to Africa.

THE mission had so far succeeded in influence, and in attracting the people to it, that more and better facilities for labor were needed. Mr. Gomer informed us that a new chapel was one of the necessities that they could not afford longer to do without. Accordingly the Executive Committee took the question under consideration, and after mature deliberation determined to order the new building immediately. Their conviction and purpose are expressed in a paper which they published in the *Religious Telescope*, November 15, 1871:

NEW CHAPEL FOR AFRICA.

One want begets another. The farmer who adds a hundred acres to his plantation soon learns that he must enlarge his barn. The missionary society have been long endeavoring to obtain a suitable and sufficient corps of missionaries for Shengay Station, West Africa. Hitherto, however, they have found it difficult to engage more than one or two at a time. Happily they now have four excellent laborers for that important field. And they were never more needed; nor were the prospects of success ever so flattering as at the present time. The gospel, in its heaven appointed power to save the souls of men, is taking fast hold of the people's hearts. Some have been already converted; others are penitently asking what they must do to be saved; and scores more are crowding to hear the word preached, asking in all sincerity: "May we know what this new doctrine whereof thou speakest, is?" What a gracious assurance the Lord is thus giving us that we have neither run nor labored in vain! Doubt and fear must now give way to security and hope. A bright, a glorious day has dawned upon our work in Africa.

But with more laborers and fairer prospects, more extensive preparations for labor must be made. It can not be avoided. We should not desire to avoid it. We ought rather to rejoice that such extended preparations are called for. David felt that it was the greatest honor that was bestowed upon him, to merely make preparations to build a house for God's worship. And Solomon, with a similar conviction, when he had completed the house his father had it in his heart to build, exclaimed: "Behold, the heaven and heaven of heavens cannot contain Thee; how much less this house that I have builded!"

We need a new chapel for our mission-station in Africa. We must have it The old chapel (made of pine wood, shipped from New York shortly after the mission was projected) was several years ago literally eaten up by the "bug-a-bug," an insect that is like a consuming fire to wooden buildings. Since it went into decay the mission-house, or residence, has been used for dwelling, school-house, and church. But it is now all occupied as a house of residence. Besides, there is no room sufficiently large, or properly arranged to accommodate the increasing numbers that are constantly seeking access to our school and church. Hence a new chapel seems to be a pressing necessity.

On considering the subject carefully, we concluded to order Mr. Gomer to proceed at once to build said chapel. There is plenty of good building-stone on the mission-grounds, and other materials can be gathered up, and a good and sufficient chapel built to serve for day-school, Sabbath-school, and church purposes, for about three thousand dollars.

But where is the money to come from? That question is certainly in order. We have no more money at our command than is necessary to support the missionaries now in the field. But as the Israelites were commanded to go forward long before they could see into Canaan, the committee felt that the Lord who owns the gold and silver, and the cattle on a thousand hills, is saying: "Build me a temple in Africa, and I will fill it with more glory than the former house," They dare not wait till they have all the money in hand. They believe that He who orders it built by the indications of His providence, will give them the money to pay for it. On this faith they have acted. They now call on the Church for a special donation for this chapel. We know that this mission has a strong hold on their affections. Special donations heretofore prove it. We now ask our brethren everywhere to send in their money in denominations of one dollar, five dollars, ten dollars, twenty dollars, fifty dollars, as they may feel able and willing to give. Many of the ministers will feel it a special privilege thus to contribute toward the evangelization of Africa. And our laymen, we trust, will cheerfully and speedily respond.

We would also request that our Sabbath-schools make a special collection for this chapel. Let the superintendents set apart a given Sabbath, explaining what the money is wanted for, and we have no doubt a liberal contribution will be the result.

J. J. Glossbrenner.
T. N. Sowers.
D. K. Flickinger.
John Kemp.
William McKee.
Executive Committee.

Dayton, O., November 15, 1871.

They did not call in vain. The churches, the Sabbath-schools, ministers and members of the Church, and of other churches, and even strangers, began to send in their money, in small sums it is true, for the most part, yet aggregating in about two years the whole amount needed.

Mr. Gomer and Mr. Evans began to collect materials, and go forward with the erection of the house. But they already had more work than they could perform satisfactorily. Accordingly the Board appointed the Rev. Peter Warner, a local minister in the Sandusky Conference, and his wife, to go to the assistance of our brethren in Africa. Mr. Warner was a carpenter as well as a minister, and after receiving ordination by Bishop Glossbrenner, at Orangeville, Ohio, he and his wife sailed from New York for Africa, on the 19th day of October, 1872, and soon arrived at Shengay.

Mr. Warner took charge of the financial interests of the mission, leaving the other missionaries free to teach and preach without interruption. Nor did he confine himself exclusively to the work of building the chapel. He frequently preached, and taught, continuing from week to week to do the work of an evangelist. The health of Mrs. Warner, however, declined rapidly; and in April, 1873, the rainy season approaching, and being unable to proceed with the building, Mr. Warner found it necessary to bring his wife to America, where he remained during the summer, recruiting his health, and waiting for the dry season, so that he might return and proceed with the chapel. In August, 1873, leaving his wife in the care of her friends, he again sailed for Africa.

The chapel which engaged his special attention, is a stone edifice, thirty-six by forty-six feet square, very substantially built, and marks an era in the history of Sherbro Mission. Nearly every man, woman, and child, connected with the United Brethren Church, is a stockholder in it, as it is probable that very few of them have failed to contribute toward the fund for its erection.

CHAPTER XXX.

Sherbro country and people—Kings' quarrels—Number of converts.

WHILE the process of building the chapel was going on, the missionaries were carrying the work into neighboring towns and provinces.

The following letter from Mr. Gomer so fully explains itself, and is withal so interesting to the Church at large, that I give it entire:

"SHENGAY, West Africa, January 9th, 1873.

" REV. D. K. FLICKINGER, Dayton, O.

"*Dear Brother*—As you request me to write you fully and freely about the work here, I shall now attempt to show you our situation at the close of 1872. I shall be as explicit as I can, showing both the encouraging and the discouraging features of the work. In my last letter to you, in reference to the work here, I closed with my return from the Turtle Islands. Bros. Evans and

Warner, as well as myself, (in fact, it was their proposition,) thought best that we give you a full statement of the country in which we are operating, geographically, politically, and religiously. Although I have been here two years, my knowledge of the country is somewhat limited.

"Native Sherbro embraces a large tract of country. South of Mr. Caulker's territory lies the Bargroo country, which is much larger than Mr. Caulker's. East of us is the Kosoo country. The tribes of both countries are very fond of war. The Bargroo country is governed by a number of chiefs, each one being independent, and making war on his neighbors whenever he chooses, which is very often. The Kosoos hold themselves in readiness to become allies to any tribe or party that may require their assistance. With a few pounds of tobacco or a few bottles of rum, or two or three pieces of cloth, two or three hundred war men can be obtained in a very short time. North of us is the Bomphe country. This is a large tract of country also. This was formerly governed by Carribaw Caulker, who died about 1859 or 1860. They had different rulers until 1864. The people then came to Shengay to Thomas Stephen Caulker, brother of Carribaw Caulker, and father of our present chief, George Caulker. They wished him to appoint them a chief. Thomas Stephen sent to Freetown to Governor Kennedy for Richard, son of the late Carribaw. Richard was being educated by the English government. He was a young man of about twenty-six or twenty-eight years of age, and had acquired a good education, and he became chief of the Bomphe country. During the next two years there were many complaints brought to Shengay against Richard. It was claimed that he treated the people badly. Mr. Caulker sent for him and he came to Shengay. The palaver was talked over, and it was determined not to send him back again. In the eastern part of the Bomphe country live a great many of the Mendi people. These are mostly Mohammedans. Richard has a brother who is a Mohammedan priest. A number of these Mohammedans slipped into Shengay, stole Richard away, and took him home again. Soon there was a rumor that he was collecting his people to bring war on Mr. Caulker, his uncle. At this the people became much frightened, and it is said that several hundred moved away to British Sherbro. This was in 1866. Since then there has been many rumors of Richard's bringing war against Mr. Caulker, and the country has ever since been in an unsettled condition. Richard and George had not met nor spoken together since, until December 23, 1872. Bannah Bandah was a sub-chief for both the Caulkers, and both of them before their death asked him to look over their children. This he pretends to be trying to do. After Carry Baw escaped from George Caulker last July, he went to the Kosoo country, and got between two and three hundred warriors. On their march here they passed through a part of Richard's country, and committed some depredations. Richard arrested them, and when they reached here Carry Baw was arrested by Bannah Bandah. Bannah Bandah was very feeble at the time, and sent for Mr. George Caulker, also to Richard and one of the most prominent Bargroo chiefs, to meet him at Genda Mah to talk the palaver. As much mischief had been done, the troubles of last July and August were also to be settled. Bannah

Bandah expects soon to die. He says he wants to see the country settled and the chiefs all on friendly terms, and then he can die in peace. The chiefs all met in October except Richard, and as he did not come, the Bargroo chief went home. George waited. On the 1st of December Richard, with between two and three hundred war men, and a great train of Murrymen and Mohammedan priests as his counsellors, arrived at Molacket, a small town on the opposite side of the river from Genda Mah. Molacket is in Richard's territory. Richard refused to cross the river to George at Genda Mah, and George refused to go over to Richard. Richard was afraid that George was playing some trick on him, and George stood on his dignity. So I think. The situation soon became known throughout the country, and all the chief men soon assembled at Genda Mah to try to effect a reconciliation between the parties, for all feared the consequences.

"On December 18th, a Mr. S. N. Lafeever, a British trader residing at Bomphe, landed at the mission on his way to the secret council. I asked and obtained passage in his boat. The next morning we were at Genda Mah. We called on Mr. Caulker and Bannah Bandah. They were very glad we had come, and hoped that we might help them out of their trouble. I knew Geooge to be very much set in his way. What he says he means, and seldom changes. I took the affair to God, and asked counsel of him, for I knew that he alone could change George's mind. At 9 o'clock the same morning we went over to Molacket. After waiting two hours we were taken from the barra to the house where Richard was. The house was surrounded with war men armed with guns and cutlasses. A strong guard was at the door. I had never seen this young chief before. Mr. Lafeever had known him from a boy. He is a fine, intelligent-looking man. He has read a great deal of history, and is very familiar with the Bible. He quotes passages freely and very correctly. I was glad of this, for I hoped to make it count for good. We spent between two and three hours with him, Mr. Lafeever doing most of the talking. He finally agreed to send his two brothers over with us, and if they were well received he would go next day. They went with us, Carribaw and Stephen. They were well received, and sent back in the evening. That night they beat drums, danced, and drank rum all night at Molacket. Next morning, December 20th, we took the boat and went over for Richard. He called his chief men together to counsel with them. I saw that they were all Mohammedans. I saw the game was up. It was useless to attempt to do anything with them. They refused to let him go; said they were his guardians, and that Bannah Bandah and Mr. Caulker must come to him. We returned to Genda Mah. George still refused to go to him.

"We proposed to start home that night, but Bannah Bandah sent to beg us to stay one more day, and make another trial. So on Saturday, the 21st, we went over to Richard again. He could do nothing without his elders' consent. He was completely under their control. The conversation turned to missions; he wanted a school in his territory. I told him we could use our money to better advantage than to establish schools where there was so strong a Mohammedan influence as I judged there must be in his country, he himself being counseled by them. He then denied being influenced by them.

"It being now about 12 o'clock Saturday, we could not reach home without traveling on the Sabbath. Mr. Lafeever proposed that we remain over and hold a meeting there on the Sabbath, and also one at Genda Mah. After what had been said Richard could not deny us this. It was agreed that we should hold a meeting at Molacket at 10 o'clock on Sunday, and in the evening at Gendah Mah.

"On the morning of the 22d, with several other traders who had collected there, we went to Molacket. I went to the house for Richard, escorted him to the barra, gave him a seat next myself, and when I began to speak asked him to interpret, which he did nicely. I read fifty seven verses of the twenty-eighth chapter of Deuteronomy, then talked from II. Corinthians v. 20; after which Mr. Lafeever spoke to the people in Shérbro. The attendance was very great, the barra and all about it being packed with people. I noticed one Murryman present at the meeting. During the meeting several others passed the barra and told Mr. Caulker good-by. And that day all the Mohamedans left Molacket. They told Mr. Caulker that they did not come there to keep the Sabbath, and if he insisted upon keeping it they would not stay. At night we had a good meeting at Genda Mah. That night there was one Mohammedan priest present. He wants an Arabic Bible that has in it about Abraham, Jacob, Joseph, Moses, and Jesus Christ. We were intending to start home between 12:00 and 1:00 A. M.; but about 9:00 P. M. a messenger came from Richard saying that all of his chief men had left him, and he must leave in the morning.

"Bannah Bandah and Mr. Caulker sent us word that if we would remain until morning they would both go over with us. We remained, and in the morning—December 23d—Mr. Caulker, with six of his chief men, and Bannah Bandah, with his staff, a number of spectators, the British traders, and myself, all went over to Molacket.

"The prisoners also were with us. Right at the wharf is a large tree, the carratt-tree. The party halted in the shade of this tree. After waiting for some time, Richard was escorted to the place by the Purrow Society. They were rigged out in all of their gorgeous trappings and paraphernalia, and made a grand display. The welkin did ring with their melody, if I may call it by that name. Bannah Bandah first shook hands with Richard; next George went to him and embraced him; and now the scene that followed, I can not describe. Several hundred persons were present, to witness the proceedings. Guns were fired, drums were beaten, and the air was filled with the shouts of the people. The women formed in companies, danced, clapped their hands, and sung songs. After the first outburst of joy was over, the two chiefs drank each other's health, in water, each making a short speech, promising that the past should all be forgotton and buried forever, and thanking us for what we had done. Other speeches were made thanking us for our services in the affair; and as all spoke either in Sherbro or Mendi, I could not understand what was being said, only as I was told. It was now about 2:00 o'clock P. M., and I must be home for Christmas. We were now ready to leave, but the people wanted we should speak to them before we left. I told them I was sorry they had made a mistake, and had thanked me for what I had done. I had only done what I knew to be my duty to do. I had said little to the chiefs. I knew that only the great God in heaven, whom I serve, was able to bring about a reconciliation. I had prayed to him, and had asked him, with my heart, to make peace between the two chiefs, and to make them good friends; and to him, and him alone, be all the praise. They must thank God. Mr. Lafeever spoke to them in Sherbro. He is a very good speaker.

"The Sabbath was observed both in Molacket and Genda Mah; but Mr. Caulker says it was the first time, and that it was only kept because the missionary was there. I met one of the head-men from Tassoh here. He attended both of our meetings. I told him that I wanted to come to Tassoh, soon to hold meeting. He said, 'Make I wait fust.'

"At 2:15 A. M., December 24th, I reached the mission, having been gone six days. Christmas night we began a protracted meeting. December 30th there were two conversions; so that, all told, up to the close of 1872 there have been forty-nine conversions. Six of these belong to the Bomphetook work, and forty-three to Shengay. There have been eighty-nine baptized. Nine of these belong to Bomphetook. Three couple have been married.

"Bro. Evans is meeting with very good success at Bomphetook and vicinity. He has four places where he preaches, namely, Coolong, Bomphetook, Manho, and Toomboo. He has made nine visits to the work, has preached thirty sermons, and there have been six conversions. He has baptized four converts and five children, has held nine seekers' meetings, besides Bible-class and visits not kept account of. Besides this, morning prayers are held, which a number of the town people attend. A chapter is read, some explanations are given, a hymn is sung, and a prayer is offered.

"One of the most discouraging features of the work here is that so many of our converts go away to other towns to live, wherever they can get work or a good place to 'make farm.' Persons are often here on a visit for a few weeks, become convicted, and are converted, but they go away. Yet I do not know that any we have counted have gone back to the world.

"Since I have been in Africa I have spoken in nineteen different towns on the subject of religion. Brother Evans and Sister Hadley have spoken in several towns. Toomboo, I think, will be a very hard place to gain converts. It is a great place for country medicine—the old chief himself being the father of the medicine. Across a river from Toomboo is a town called Bendoo. The last time I was at Toomboo I sent word to the headman of Bendoo that I wished to see him. When he came, I told him I wished to 'keep' meeting in his town that day. He said I must make cannana first. I had nothing to give him, so I held no meeting there. But many of his people came over to Toomboo to meeting.

"We try to avoid getting up religious excitements to bring people into the Church. My belief is that they make much better members and do more credit to the cause of Christ if they are brought into the Church during a calm. We are careful for the reputation of the Church throughout the country here. People have the greatest reverence for the mission and the missionaries. Several who profess religion have not yet been baptized nor joined the believers' class. Up to the close of the year eighty-nine have been baptized. Thirty-one of these are children; yet several of them have been converted, being twelve and fourteen years of age. The minutes of the Sabbath-school have not been kept regularly, but the average for the year, I think, we may put at fifty. During the rains the attendance is small. We are now having in the Sabbath-school from seventy to one hundred and twenty-five. This is the highest. Thomas says the average for the day-school is thirty. Since New-years the attendance has been from forty-two to sixty-two; but when the rains begin, many of these children will be taken out of school, to drive birds off the rice. One of the female converts was here from Bomphetook, the other day. She told me that she could not thank God too much for bringing the gospel there; 'that day when Mr. Evans tell her he is coming again, she can look all day till she see the boat, then her heart can glad; she hope God can bless all them people in America what send the gospel to we.'

"Taking all things into consideration, I think the work here is very encouraging. Ethiopia is stretching forth her hands, and God is not slack concerning his promises.

"To-day is the 21st of January, 1873. I hope soon to have an opportunity to send this letter to you. We closed our protracted meeting on the 10th. The result was, nineteen conversions. Sabbath, the 19th, Bros. Evans and Warner baptized forty-two—sixteen adults and twenty-six children. At night, forty-one partook of the Lord's-supper, and seventeen joined the believers' class. These are now on the believers' class-book. And so the work goes on. To God be all the glory.

"For myself and my wife, I can say that we are contented and happy in our work. I received a letter from Dayton a few days ago, asking if I did not wish myself back again in Dayton. No one need have any such apprehensions. I never was as well contented and as happy in a situation as I am here. Every day I can point sinners to the Lamb of God; every day I can assist in tearing down the strong works of the enemy of my heavenly Father and my Redeemer. I am fighting under the banner of the King of Glory, who never lost a battle. In every contest we are sure of the victory. The enemy is flying before us. I wish to stay here to possess the land. This is a glorious warfare, and I wish to remain and see the end of the battle; and if you will pray for it, God will work yet greater wonders here in Africa, for we are told that he will withhold no good thing from them that walk uprightly. Remember us to all friends.

"At 6 A. M., on Sabbath, we have class; at 11:00, preaching; at 2:00 P. M., Sabbath-school; at 7:00, preaching. Tuesday night we have Bible-class, Wednesday night, prayer-meeting, and on Friday night, seekers' meeting. We are visiting and talking with the people every day."

Brother Gomer adds, in a note dated January 24th, 1873:

"My letter is not gone yet, and, as I have a few spare moments, I will scratch off a few lines more, for I suppose you wish to know of all our movements. Our protracted meeting closed on the 10th. On the 11th Bro. Warner and wife and Sister Hadley returned from town. Bro. Warner had fever. On the 14th,—he being better,—himself, wife, Mrs. Hadley, and myself, started up the Cockburrow. I had engaged some lumber up the river. I went with him to see the parties. I also wished to see the two chiefs. They are now the very best of friends. Their war troubles are all being adjusted, and it looks as though the country was going to be in a more settled condition than ever. On the night of the 15th we held a meeting at Bwarlille. We had left an appointment at Molacket, for the 16th; but the big palaver was decided about 5 o'clock P. M., and there was such an uproar in the town that it was useless to attempt to hold a meeting. So we passed on to the mission. We reached home on the 17th.

"I should have sent this report sooner, but I wished to copy it; and then I have spent much time with the young converts. They need and must have good attention, for they have much to contend with here, and we can not afford to lose one of them. Our meetings are so conducted that we can keep up a seekers' class all the time, and have conversions right along.

"On the 25th, the Lord willing, my wife and I expect to go to Bomphetook to spend a few weeks, and it may be some time before I write you again.

"I wish we had a few Arabic Bibles. The

half dozen that I brought with me are gone, and I hope that some, at least, are doing good.

"There are many things that I should like to write, but already my letter is very tedious. So I close by saying, Pray for the success of Zion in Africa. We will trust in God for success."

CHAPTER XXXI.
Closing Remarks.

THE year 1873 witnessed the continued prosperity of our mission among the Sherbroes. Mr. Gomer and his wife continued to enjoy unusually good health for that climate, and to labor with unabated zeal for the spread of the gospel. Mrs. Hadley, too, remained at her post during the entire year, retaining the fullest confidence of the people, and teaching and preaching the kingdom of God to them for whom she has shown herself ready to suffer the loss of all things, so that she might both win Christ herself and win the people to Christ. Early in the year Mr. Warner, finding that Mrs. Warner could not endure the climate, returned with her to America, and remained during the continuance of the rainy season in Africa, returning again in September to finish the stone chapel, and in other ways help to forward the interests of the mission. Mr. Evans, on the call of the Board, returned to America in August, and took charge of a home mission in the Shennadoah Valley, Virginia.

The General Conference which met in May, 1873, had abundant reason to thank God that they had four years ago ordered the Board "to keep the door wide open" for missionary labor in Africa. They heard with unmixed satisfaction, not of decaying buildings and dying hopes in Africa, and at home an empty treasury, no missionaries, and little disposition on the part of the Church to furnish either men or means to carry on the only foreign mission under the care of the Board; but instead, of new buildings, and, what was of far more consequence, of living stones gathered for the spiritual temple of the Lord Jesus in Africa; that Ethiopia was stretching her hands to God, and that God was receiving and saving them from sin and death; they heard that men and women were ready to go at the bidding of the Board, even to Africa, for the purpose of building up the Redeemer's kingdom; and that the Church was both by her prayers and contributions saying to the Board, "Go forward." What a contrast to the report they were compelled to hear four years previously! There was now no debate or hesitancy about the Sherbro Mission. Success is a great support to the faith of even good Christians.

The Church of the United Brethren in Christ, as a separate denomination, is now one hundred years old. It counts one hundred and twenty-five thousand souls in actual membership, and as many more who are devotedly attached to her, and as anxious for her prosperity, apparently, as if their names were on her rolls. And she has millions of treasure as well as grand opportunities, both at home and abroad, to spend it in extending the Redeemer's kingdom. She now employs three hundred missionaries in all the home, frontier, and foreign fields. If true to her trust, who can tell how many she may employ one hundred years hence! This, then, is a fitting period to close the history of Sherbro mission, or rather, I might say, the history of the origin of the mission, for it is yet in its infancy. God grant that at the end of another score of years instead of one hundred converts they may be numbered by the thousand. Have we not every reason to hope for it? The gospel is the power of God unto salvation. The history of the missions in India, and Madagascar Island, and the Sandwich Islands, and the promises of God's own word confirm our faith. We have been sowing the seed for twenty years. The harvest is ripe, and already our missionaries are gathering the sheaves.

MISSION IN GERMANY.

CHAPTER I.

WHEN the General Conference was held in Lebanon, Pennsylvania, May, 1869, there was developed a strong desire to project another foreign mission. Since the establishment of Sherbro Mission the Church had increased one half in members and wealth, and it was believed she was not only able; but anxious to have the privilege to support another foreign mission. The German delegates were especially anxious to unfurl our banner in Germany. They maintained that we could more cheaply and more speedily win souls there than in any other foreign country. It was easily reached by well established lines of travel, the missionaries would speak the language of the people, and without the tedious preliminary process necessary in most foreign countries they could immediately commence the work of evangelists. Moreover, the mission would soon become a valuable recruiting station. The ship loads of immigrants wending their way to our shores would contain a greater or less number of souls who had been won to Christ by the labors of our missionaries; and these would very naturally seek a home with us in this country. These and other considerations prompted the Board to make an appropriation for the establishment of a mission in Germany, and to charge the Executive Committee with the duty of securing and appointing a missionary to that important field.

Shortly after the committee appointed Rev. C. Bischoff, of Zanesville, Ohio, and in September, 1869, he sailed for Germany. As had been expected, he found an open door. The people were anxious to hear the word of life. In a few months he reported quite a number of souls converted and a society organized. It was not like going among a heathen people. They were educated. They read and believed the Bible. They only wanted some one whose lips were touched with a live coal from the altar to teach them the doctrine of a present, free, full, experimental salvation. Formalism and ritualism, a cold and lifeless style of theorizing, which had no power to stir men's souls to conviction or to lead them to the great Physician, had taken possession of the pulpit in Germany. Hence it was that the people were settled down in a state of deadness and irreligion little better than that which preceded the Reformation headed by Luther and Melancthon. When, therefore, instead of the uncertain sounds of these faithless shepherds, or dead dogs, our missionary began in the simplicity and earnestness of a faithful embassador of the cross to cry out, "Oh, wicked man, thou shalt die!" "Except ye repent, ye shall all likewise perish!" the people soon began to ask, "Sir, what must we do to be saved?" Being told, they belived and were saved. As one after another tasted of the good word of God and the powers of the world to come they naturally flowed together. They were travelers seeking a better country, and sought company and fellowship one with another. Consequently they organized a "society"—they dared not call it "church,"—

which in less than one year numbered nearly one hundred souls. When the Board met, one year after the General Conference, they gave expression to their gratification in the following:

"*Resolved*, That we are highly gratified to learn that our missionary to Germany has been eminently successful. As the results of his labors for the past year, seventy-two have been brought into the Church. We recommend that the Executive Committee make arrangements to send one additional missionary to Germany as soon as practicable."

Before the committee had secured the missionary the terrible war which involved not only Prussia, but all the German states, in a deadly conflict with France, was already begun. For a time little else was thought of or attempted by the people. They rallied to the standard of the fatherland as one man, and for a short time it looked like our missionary would apparently lose the ground he had already gained. But though the work was hindered, it was not abandoned. Mr. Bischoff continued to labor; and amid the excitement, confusion, cost, and blood of a great war between two powerful nations, the truth still found a lodging in the hearts of the people. The committee, of course, deemed it not advisable in this state of the national affairs to send any more missionaries. And when the Board met, in August, 1871, the war cloud having well nigh passed away, they gave expression to their feelings by the passage of the following resolution:

"We have abundant cause for devout gratitude to God that notwithstanding the unfavorable influences resulting from the recent great war between Germany and France, the success and present condition of our mission in Germany is favorable.

"We have, by the success already realized by this mission, unmistakable indications of the approbation of God upon this special work, as well as the clearest promptings to greater and more vigorous efforts in the future. We recommend that another missionary be sent to reënforce Bro. Bischoff as soon as practicable, and that the Executive Committee be empowered to appropriate to it whatever amount may be deemed necessary."

After casting about for some time the committee appointed the Rev. Jacob Ernst and his wife as missionaries to Germany.

This gentleman, though born in Germany, had been a resident of America for many years. He and his family were strongly attached to the free institutions of their adopted country. He had also been recently settled over a German congregation in Toledo, Ohio, and was just beginning to feel at home when the Board called on him to accept an appointment to Bavaria. After considering the question most prayerfully he concluded that he would return to his native country, and do what he could to bring his fellow-countrymen to the knowledge of Christ crucified. Accordingly he sailed from New York on the 7th of December, 1872, and in due time arrived safely in the land of his nativity.

CHAPTER II.

PREVIOUS to the arrival of Mr. Ernst, Mr. Bischoff had received twenty-six additional members into the society, making about one hundred in all.

Our work had now so far progressed and the prospect for the future was so good that our missionaries thought they could no longer go on without a legally organized church. Bavaria has a state church, and it is a penal offense to establish another without the consent of the king; and, besides all this, the want of authority from the ruler subjected them to the jeers and persecutions of the multitude, many of whom, though regular church-members, were utterly destitute of the grace that brings salvation, and very bigoted and intolerant withal, not willing to allow any freedom of utterance or enjoyment on the part of those who differed in faith or practice from the state church.

Accordingly our missionaries presented a

petition to the king, including the confession of faith, constitution, and all the essential parts of our Discipline, asking the consent of the Crown to establish a United Brethren Church in Bavaria. Pending the consideration of this petition by the king, the General Conference of 1873 assembled, and Mr. Bischoff came all the way from Germany to attend it. And it was well he did. The conference seemed to be inclined to think our missionaries had been entirely too forward in presenting this petition. Some, however, thought it would have been well, had not fragments of the Discipline been left out of the petition. Still others believed they ought to have waited till authorized by the General Conference, or at least by the Board of Missions, before taking this step. Considerable discussion ensued. The part of the report of the Committee on Missions which recommeded that Mr. Bischoff's proceedings be adopted, was finally referred to a special committee consisting of the Board of Bishops and Dr. Davis. The next day they reported in favor of adopting the recommendation of the Mission Committee, and the conference without opposition approved the report.

As the petition presented to the king is rather a unique document I herewith present it to my readers:

PETITION TO THE KING OF BAVARIA.

"*His most serene highness, most powerful king, most gracious king and lord.*

"NAILA, March 11, 1873.

"*Most obedient presentation and prayer of Christian Bischoff and associates of Naila, for the most gracious permission of building a religious association under the name of "United Brethren in Christ in the Kingdom of Bavaria."*

"For several years many persons of the Lower Naila and vicinity have felt that the word of God alone can give life and happiness. After a thorough search, we found, as your most obedient and true servants, that the lives of thousands of men are not in accordance but contrary to the word of God.

"The consciences of the better part of men, by the word of God awakened more and more, and also sought to lead better lives, and by the help of God continue therein.

"These persons did get more and more acquainted with one another, and as they sought one point, and to serve our Lord, they did build a society, which they named "Christian Association at Naila." They sought (and it was granted to them) the permission of the king's court, in 1870.

"These simple private meetings were, to many persons, a blessing, and, therefore, they found it necessary and convenient to assemble together, as such who will try to serve our Lord, for they were of one heart and one mind.

"The Lord God now gave the chance that Christian Bischoff went to America, where he lived for several years, and where he was thoroughly converted to Him who died for him. Soon he felt the impression on his mind to preach Christ and him crucified, and he was licensed to preach the gospel among the United Brethren in Christ, as his inclosed license of ordination will also show, and as such he returned to Naila, in Bavaria.

"When he returned, he still found the small flock which he had left several years previously, anxious to work out their salvation with fear and trembling, and he soon joined them as leader, to which he was appointed May 31st, 1870.

"They now held their own meetings, and the Lord blest them abundantly, and many were converted to God. They declared that they would not erect a different church, but would stay as a society, provided they would not hinder them in their meetings.

"It was soon found that they must extend their association, for there were more people who would come and assemble with them, and, therefore, they asked for more liberty to hold their meetings. But then they were threatened by the clergy, as well as by several ruffians, and it was tried to hinder them in assembling together. They therefore appealed to the court to establish a "home mission of the United Brethren in Christ in the kingdom of Bavaria;" but this was refused to them on the 18th of January, 1873, for the following reasons:

"(*a*.) As C. Bischoff would do such things as were only allowed to the clergy of the Lutheran Church of Bavaria, as preaching the gospel and teaching religious doctrines to old and young, administering the sacraments, &c.

"(*b*.) As his actions plainly show that he will not only be the leader of a small congregation,—as he expressed himself,—but to preach and teach doctrines contrary to the Lutheran Church, and so establish another religious body, namely, the United Brethren in Christ, of America.

"(c.) To this the law requires that they must have the consent of his majesty the king, according to sections 26 and 27; and therefore they must take this step to be allowed to have their own society. They have, according to law, made their wishes known to the pastor of the Lutheran Church, which they so long delayed, and also to the Court of Naila, that they wish to dissolve their former connection as a little class of brethren and sisters in the Lutheran Church.

"Although they acted strictly according to law, they were notified that if they should further assemble together to hold religious meetings, they would be fined fifteen dollars, as the law states.

"Therefore, the undersigned most obedient servants of your most esteemed highness, the King of Bavaria, are compelled to withdraw from the Lutheran Church, which they have done. They now stand alone, without any spiritual food in the church which they so much need; and they desire to build up their own society,—a society with the doctrines and confessions of faith which your majesty will find annexed to this petition. We would most obediently pray your most gracious majesty, the most serene highness the King of Bavaria, to grant to us your most gracious permission to establish a Church of the United Brethren in Christ in the Kingdom of Bavaria."

[Signed by the Petitioners.]

I regret that my book goes to press before learning whether the king has granted the request of the petitioners.

HOME MISSIONS.

CHAPTER I.

Origin of the Missionary Society.

AS it may be several years before a history proper of our home and frontier mission work will be offered to the Church, it has been deemed best to present a brief statement of these departments of our mission work in this volume. To do this satisfactorily in the space alloted is a rather difficult task. Nevertheless it is believed that an increased degree of usefulness, the chief object aimed at by its publication, will be given the volume by this supplement.

The Missionary Society of the Church of the United Brethren in Christ was organized by the General Conference which assembled in the month of May, 1853, in Miltonville, Butler County, Ohio.

But the reader must not suppose for a moment that this Church was not engaged in the missionary enterprise prior to this date. Nearly all the annual conferences had their missions, made annual collections, and, within their own territorial limits, expended their labor and their money. The time had now come when all felt that an efficient missionary organization was demanded alike by the wants of the church at large and those who were without the gospel. It was not deemed quite right or in keeping with the teachings of God's word to confine our efforts exclusively to the limits of the annual conferences. Hence the organization of the Missionary Society with the avowed purpose of "aiding the annual conferences in extending their missionary labors throughout the country and into foreign and heathen lands."

The design of this supplement is to show as nearly as possible what these annual conferences have been enabled in the last twenty years to do inside their own territorial limits, and in building up the Church in other sections of the country under the management of the Missionary Society. It will be observed that the parent Board is merely the aggregate of which each annual conference is a part, having a branch secretary and a branch treasurer of the Missionary Society. Thus the whole Church is linked together in a society for the purpose of concentrating its forces and so disposing of them as to accomplish far better results than could be hoped for by the independent and fragmentary efforts put forth by each annual conference.

When the Missionary Society was organized there were only fourteen annual conferences, namely: Pennsylvania, East Pennsylvania, Virginia, Alleghany, Scioto, Miami, Muskingum, Sandusky, Illinois, Wabash, Indiana, White River, St. Joseph, and Iowa.

The whole number of members in the Church at this period did not exceed fifty thousand. The Miltonville General Conference took the question of a missionary society under consideration, and after mature deliberation gave the Church a constitution so well adapted to its wants that few changes have been required in it during the score of years it has been in operation; a high compliment to the sagacity and forethought of the ministers composing said body.

Before attempting to describe the organization and practical workings of the Board itself I will note a few of the movements of the annual conferences immediately preceding the organization of the Missionary Society.

For several years the conferences were thinking and praying for the more rapid spread of the truth, and striving, each in its own way and time, to build up the Master's kingdom. A number of them organized themselves into home missionary societies for the purpose of systematizing and more rapidly advancing the work of evangelization. Scioto and Muskingum conferences led off in this good work, in 1838. The Virginia Conference followed in 1839, and the Alleghany in 1840. The General Conference, held in 1841, appointed a missionary Board, but it would seem made no definite arrangements for the line of policy, if indeed it had any plan or outline of a policy, for the Board to pursue. The consequence was, the Board did nothing. The General Conference of 1845, however, appointed another Board, which followed in its predecessor's steps very closely. It did nothing; it undertook nothing. Four years more of inactivity did not suffice to open the eyes either of the Board or the General Conference. The General Conference assembled again in 1849, and so easy is it for an assembly of men, as well as an individual, to move on in a well-marked groove, that they again elected a Board of Missions without giving it a constitution or pointing out particularly what it was expected to do, or by what method it might accomplish the work. Four years more passed. By this time the pent up zeal of the annual conferences could no longer be restrained. The Miltonville General Conference gave to the Missionary Society a constitution, elected officers charged with specific duties, and placed behind them a Board of Directors. Now the work began to move on in earnest.

But previous to this the annual conferences were not idle. The Sandusky Conference, as early as 1840, had formed a few classes in the State of Michigan. The good work increased as the years wore away, until at the time of the organization of the Missionary Society in 1853, the classes and circuits in the State of Michigan were set apart as a mission-conference, having eleven preachers and several hundred members.

The German ministers were also actively engaged. They had commenced preaching in a goodly number of towns and cities in different portions of the country, and had organized a great many churches. In the prosecution of their work they received some support from individuals and from conferences, though most of them labored at a heavy personal sacrifice. When the General Conference of 1853 assembled, these churches were in a healthy, growing condition, and were consequently set apart as a separate annual conference.

The Miami Conference also manifested a commendable zeal in missionary work. After the division of the territory originally known as the Miami Conference, in 1853, giving the south-eastern portion of the State of Ohio to the Scioto Conference, there had been several conferences organized in territory that had been known under the general name of Miami. The Indiana, and the Auglaize, may be mentioned, the last named being disconnected from the old conference by the General Conference which assembled in 1853.

The Sandusky Conference, which was begun by the Muskingum Conference in 1829, had grown to large proportions by the meeting of the General Conference in 1853. The Bevers, Brights, Lillibridges, Longs, and other ministers whose names were towers of strength, had built up a flourishing conference, which as to members, wealth, and intelligence had become one of the first in the whole denomination. It took a leading part in diffusing the principles which led to the organization of the Missionary Society. At the annual conference in 1852, a committee, of which the Rev. J. C. Bright was chairman, made in substance the following report on missions, which was unanimously adopted by the conference:

I. That the time has now come when the United Brethren Church should unite her whole strength in a Missionary Society, which shall include not only the home but the frontier and foreign fields within the sphere of its labors.

II. That the Sandusky Conference organize itself into a branch missionary society, with the prayer that the General Conference will form a general society, of which each conference may be a branch.

III. That the payment of one dollar shall constitute a person a member of the society for one year; ten dollars, a life member; and fifty dollars, a life director.

IV. That our brethren be entreated to exercise the most prayerful thought and careful inquiry into the wants of the nominally Christian, and especially heathen world, that their views may be enlarged in regard to the magnitude of the work devolving upon the Christian church, in fulfilling the commission given by our Savior on the mount, just before his ascension.

After this the reader will not wonder that, as the General Conference so closely followed the principles enunciated in these resolutions, it should elect the Rev. J. C. Bright for its first corresponding secretary. He was a man of decided ability and unusual zeal, well qualified for the duties of the position, and he soon infused his own spirit, in a large measure, into the hearts of hundreds of ministers and laymen.

Shortly after the territory of Oregon was opened to settlers, a number of United Brethren families from the eastern part of the Union, removed to the new territory where, in addition to other privations incident to pioneer life, they were entirely destitute of the ministrations of God's house. In this state of spiritual destitution they wrote several very touching appeals to the ministers and members of the Church in the East. These appeals were published in the *Religious Telescope*, and widely read. They produced the impression everywhere that the Church in some way ought to send missionaries to that distant land, and that, too, without delay. After a short time, Rev. T. J. Conner, of the White River Conference, suggested through the church organ the propriety of making up a colony of United Brethren families, among them as many preachers as could be enlisted, to emigrate to Oregon and make it their permanent home. The suggestion was well received, and in due course of time the colony, including Mr. Conner and his family, and Rev. J. Kenoyer, also of White River Conference, were *en route* for Oregon Territory, by the overland route. This was in 1853, so that they were on the way at the very time the Miltonville General Conference was in session.

No one but the members of the colony knows, or can know, what hardships and sufferings they endured before reaching their destination. However, after a tedious and perilous journey they at length found a home in the new territory, the ministers supporting themselves and their families, for the most part, with the labor of their own hands, and at the same time serving as shepherds over the flock of God in that vast wilderness. The church in the East did not pay more than half their expenses, and the colonists could do no more than take care of themselves.[1]

It may be added here that the White River and the Sciota Conferences were not only first in urging the colony to emigrate to Oregon, but they furnished most of the money by which the missionaries were sent and sustained for the first year after their arrival.

Mr. Conner and Mr. Kenoyer labored amid many discouragements, but God owned their labors, and in a comparatively short time they began to organize churches and group them together so as to form missions and circuits. In his first report to the Board, received by Mr. Bright in July, 1853, Mr Conner wrote that he had not been able to find more than sixty members of the United Brethren Church in Oregon, including the colony that accompanied him. This was but a small beginning; but God does not despise the day of small things, and He soon caused the Oregon brethren to experience the truth of the assertion that He can work by many or by few. The demands for preaching were many and pressing, and in a comparatively brief period, as we shall see, it grew to be quite a flourishing Conference.

Let us recapitulate: In 1853 the United Brethren Church numbered fifty thousand communicants, and probably four hundred itinerant and three hundred local preachers. These figures are as nearly correct as can be now obtained. They are sufficiently accurate for all practical purposes. These members and ministers were included in fourteen annual conferences. But, as already shown, four new conferences were set apart at this time, namely: The Ohio German, the Michigan, the Auglaize, and the Oregon. But these new conferences did not increase the number of members or ministers, all of whom were included in the previous reckoning.

Such is a brief statement of the numbers in the United Brethren Church in 1853.

Of the HOME, FRONTIER, AND FOREIGN MISSIONARY SOCIETY, J. J. Glossbrenner, senior bishop of the Church, was elected president;

Rev. H. Kumler, jr., Rev. D. Edwards, and Rev. L. Davis, vice-presidents; Rev. J. C. Bright, corresponding secretary; Rev. John Kemp, jr., treasurer; Rev. Wm. Longstreet, Rev. D. Shuck, T. N. Sowers, Esq., Rev. D. B. Crouse, and John Dodds, Esq., managers or board of directors.

The corresponding secretary gave himself immediately to the work. He traveled extensively, preached and lectured incessantly, wrote private letters, and published frequent and stirring appeals to the Church at large, and to the annual conferences. Such efforts produced their proper fruits. The Church began to move. It could not but feel that something more thorough and aggressive than it had ever yet undertaken, must be begun and carried on with a degree of zeal corresponding to its numbers and wealth, if it wished to retain its good name among the evangelical churches of the land.

CHAPTER II.

MISSION CONFERENCES—STATISTICS.

THE twelfth General Conference convened in Hartsville, Indiana, in May, 1857. The cause of missions was working more effectually than the most sanguine could have hoped four years before. A number of new conferences were either already organized, or waited the bidding of the General Conference to become organized parts of the Church at large.

CANADA CONFERENCE.

The mission work in Canada, under the lead of that indefatigable laborer, the Rev. I. Sloan, formerly of the Scioto Conference, had so increased in fact, and presented such an inviting future that an annual conference was organized by Bishop Glossbrenner, April 19, 1856. The new conference numbered six itinerant preachers, and a membership of 152. They had strong faith, a broad and inviting field, and the command of the Master, "Go into my vineyard and work."

The corresponding secretary, Mr. Bright, reported that the Canada Conference, up to the period of its organization had cost the Board of Missions, $1,709.43. But the infant conference had already paid to the Board of Missions and to their own missionaries $1,076.57, so that, as a matter of fact, the Canada Conference had only cost the Board $633.43! It now had a membership of 400, and was in a flourishing condition.

KANSAS CONFERENCE.

Missionary operations had also been commenced in Kansas. Rev. S. S. Snyder and Rev. John Ginerich, of the Alleghany, and Rev. W. A. Cardwell, of the White River Conference, were the first missionaries sent to this fair, young territory. Having a mild climate, a soil of unsurpassed fertility, and immigrants pouring into it by the thousand it was supposed to be a very inviting missionary field Alas, for human expectations! It proved for several years to be the theater of strife and bloodshed. It was not yet determined whether it should be a free or a slave state. The immigrants from the South were resolved that its fair plains should be set apart for the expansion and rapid growth of the "peculiar institution," as slavery was fondly termed by the South, and the immigrants from the North were equally determined that this noble territory should be consecrated to freedom. I need not recount the struggle that ensued. What with the insolence of southern immigrants, backed by rich slaveholders in the states, a Supreme Court that declared " that negroes had no rights that white men are bound to respect," and a President in the chair at Washington thoroughly allied to the slaveholding interests, and as thoroughly determined to force upon the unwilling citizens of Kansas a pro-slavery constitution, our missionaries found it was very difficult soil to cultivate. At this period Mr. Bright wrote: "The *political* sky in Kansas is a little cloudy at present, but freedom must, in the end, prevail. And if Kansas should even be a slave state, we ought not, on that account, abandon it. Oh, no! The gospel of Christ is LIGHT, and wherever the dark cloud of slavery is spread, there should the gospel light be diffused."

Our brethren, however, had counted the cost and were determined not to be foiled by trifles, or even the most powerful impediments that men and devils might oppose to their progress. They were, indeed, sometimes "troubled on every side, yet not distressed; perplexed, but not in despair; persecuted, but not forsaken; cast down, but not destroyed;" and as they went forth weeping, bearing precious seed, God caused it to take root and grow, so that the General Conference set apart that portion of the mission work for a new conference. Accordingly Bishop Edwards visited the state and organized the Kansas Conference, October 30, 1857. There were nine itinerant preachers and 196 members. So much for faith and perseverance in the cause of freedom, and of the evangelization of the people.

MINNESOTA CONFERENCE.

This conference was set apart by the General Conference in May of 1857, and organized by Bishop L. Davis in the autumn of the same year. It had three itinerants at that time, namely, Rev. J. W. Fulkerson, Rev. E. Clow, and Rev. John Haney, and a membership of nearly two hundred. A scarcity of laborers was then, and has always been, the crying want of the Minnesota Conference. Nevertheless we have always had a few earnest and most faithful itinerants in that new and flourishing state, nowithstanding the severity of the climate, and the tendency of the people to Congregationalism. The conference was now fairly established, and we shall take pleasure in recording its progress from time to time. Meantime we turn to the

MISSOURI CONFERENCE.

This state has been the theater of the labors and some prosperity for a number of missionaries. In the south-western part of the state considerable effort was put forth and a mission-conference organized by Bishop D. Edwards in November, 1854. There were five preachers and as many fields of labor. But the excitement on the slavery question, "border ruffianism," and the hatred to the United Brethren Church by slaveholders, on account of her testimony against the institution of slavery, well nigh extinguished the work in that part of the state. True, the ministers clung tenaciously to their convictions and to the Church of their choice, and many of the members still preserved their integrity, but our preachers were compelled to leave the country and seek homes elsewhere.

But while the work seemed to be suspended in the southern, the good seed was being sown by some of the ministers of the Des Moines Conference in the northern part of Missouri, and the General Conference of 1857 recommended the organization of a new conference at an early day. In the fall of 1858 Bishop Edwards had the pleasure of organizing said body with a membership of 358, and nine fields of labor. They held another conference next spring, after an interval of only five months, and found that the membership had increased to 809. This was a very fair beginning, and the conference has continued to increase ever since.

WISCONSIN CONFERENCE.

The first mission work in the State of Wisconsin by the United Brethren Church was begun by ministers from Illinois, chief among them Rev. James Davis. The General Conference of 1857, learning of the work in that state, ordered a separate conference to be organized as soon as practicable. Accordingly Bishop Davis met the preachers in Dane County, in the fall of 1858, and organized a conference of twenty-one preachers, and supplied as many fields of labor. The number of members was reported at 554.

PARKERSBURG CONFERENCE.

At the same General Conference the Parkersburg Conference was set off from the Virginia Conference. It is located in West Virginia. One year after their organization they reported a membership of 1,894. Salary paid the preachers, $1,404.92.

KENTUCKY MISSION-CONFERENCE.

Rev. A. Armstrong and Rev. W. Blair, two very devoted ministers whom God raised up to preach in this state, reported six preachers, nine meeting houses, and three fields of labor. The General Conference therefore recognized it as one of its own children, and set it off as a conference to be organized by one of the bishop's at an early day.

It will thus be seen that in four years after the organization of the Missionary Society there were added to the Church, Oregon, Kansas, Missouri, Minnesota, Wisconsin,

Kentucky, Parkersburg, and Canada conferences. True, they were not yet all organized at the meeting of the General Conference, but they were already in existence, in fact some of them were actually organized, and others only waited for a formal recognition by the bishop.

The expenditures of the Board for the whole field for the first quadrennial term will be seen by the following

TABLE.

Oregon Conference	$ 3,420 00	
Kansas Conference	2,550 00	
Missouri Conference	1,750 00	
Ohio German Conference	2,950 00	
Michigan Conference	1,200 00	
Minnesota Conference	400 00	
Canada Conference	2,401 00	
Nebraska Missions	1,500 00	
Total for frontier work		$16,171 00
Sherbro Mission, West Africa		5,500 00
Home missions		60,102 42

MISCELLANEOUS EXPENSES.

Salaries for the four years	$1350 00	
Traveling and other expenses	366 96	
Printing annual reports, certificates, &c.	524 34	
Total		2,240 40
Total expenditures of the society for the quadrennial term ending April 30, 1857.		$84,013 82

The foregoing table shows that the annual

conferences, instead of diminishing their efforts in the home work by the assistance they gave to the frontier and foreign fields, were actually quickened into far greater activity, thus verifying the proverb, "The liberal soul shall be made fat: and he that watereth shall be watered also himself."

The bishops' address to the conference showed that there were now 449 itinerant and 417 local preachers, in all 866. The membership of the Church had swelled to 61,399, an increase of 6,044 members in one year, and a gain in the four years of 11,399. There were now twenty-two annual conferences, a gain of eight in four years.

Such is a statement of the condition and prospects of the United Brethren Church, in its home and frontier mission work in May, 1857.

CHAPTER III.

Organization of Nebraska Conference—General Statistics.

THE thirteenth General Conference was held in Westerville, Ohio, in May, 1861. There were now thirty conferences in the Church, including those which had been recognized by the preceding General Conference, and one or two which had been organized without any special order from that body, namely:

Virginia, Pennsylvania, East Pennsylvania, Alleghany, Parkersburg, Scioto, Miami, Muskingum, Erie, Sandusky, Auglaize, Ohio German, Canada, Michigan, Indiana, White River, St. Joseph, Upper Wabash, Lower Wabash, Illinois, Rock River, Wisconsin, Minnesota, Iowa, Des Moines, Missouri, Kansas, Canada, Kentucky, and Oregon. There were no delegates from Oregon or Kentucky. The presiding bishops were J. Russel, J. J. Glossbrenner, D. Edwards, and L. Davis.

NEBRASKA CONFERENCE.

This work had grown into some consequence under the faithful labors of Rev. J. M. Dosh, and in the autumn of 1858 Bishop Edwards visited the territory and organized the Nebraska Conference. It maintained its existence, but its growth was rather slow. At the meeting of the General Conference in 1861, its statistics showed that it had eight classes and 135 members, five Sabbath-schools and 160 scholars. A lack of laborers appears to have been the chief cause of delay in the Nebraska mission work.

The tables following will give the reader a better understanding of the Missionary Society's operations in the frontier than could otherwise be obtained.

The New England mission referred to on next page was projected, and thus far supported by the Sandusky Conference. On the 7th of February, 1859, Bishop Davis dedicated the first United Brethren chapel in Massachusetts.

I find it very difficult to obtain reliable statistics. In fact it is utterly impossible to trace all the details of the home missionary operations.

HOME MISSIONS.

STATISTICAL TABLE.

Mission-Conferences and Missions	Missionary Collection in 1861	Salary of Preachers in 1861	Missionary Collection in 1857	Salary of Preachers in 1857	Church-members in 1861	Church-members in 1857	Money Collected for S. S. Purposes in 1861	S. S. Scholars in 1861
Parkersburg Conference	$56 34	$1446 32			2,210		$34 25	907
Canada Conference	432 16	867 96			703	400	49 00	395
Missouri Conference	46 85	983 75			1,001	146	32 00	299
Oregon Conference	38 94	568 83			573	500		
Kansas Conference			$1076 57	$7 00	928			
Wisconsin Conference			20 00	500 00	1,885			
Ohio German Conference		2868 50	50 00		1,218			
Kentucky Conference					400	97		
Minnesota Conference	133 51				600			
Nebraska Conference	939 34				220			
Tennessee Missions					120			
New England Missions					100			
California Missions					50			
Totals	$1828 14	$8755 37	$1146 57	$507 00	10,008	1143	$115 35	1601

The field of labor which was occupied as a mission one year, became self-supporting the next, and was dropped from the list of "missions," and the field served as a circuit one year was divided the next, thus making two missions, or one self-supporting work and one mission. All, therefore, that can be done toward showing the statistics of the home work, is to give the aggregates as published by the bishops at the General Conferences. And, on the whole, this may be more satisfactory to the reader than a lengthy tabular statement, which, in the nature of things, must be very imperfect up to the year 1861.

THE BISHOPS' ADDRESS

To the General Conference in 1861 contained the following statistics:

Preaching places	5,166
Classes	3,900
Members	94,453
Itinerant preachers 417	
Local preachers ....1041—	1,458
Meeting-houses	1,041
Sabbath-schools	1,513
Increase in four years of classes	1,284
Increase of members	33,054
Increase of meeting-houses	267
Increase of Sabbath-schools	504

The quadrennial report of the corresponding secretary contained the following statistics:

Expenditures for Sherbro Mission in four years..	$7,349 67

FRONTIER WORK.

For Canada Conference in four years	3,550 00
For Michigan Conference	500 00
For Wisconsin Conference	900 00
For Minnesota Conference	2,020 00
For Nebraska Conference	1,755 00
For Kansas Conference	2,750 00
For Missouri Conference	1,350 00
For Tennessee Conference	731 25
For Parkersburg Conference	873 03
For German Mission-conference...............$	3,700 00
For California	50 00
Oregon	3,293 09
Total........$	28,822 04
Salaries paid Missionaries.........$	16,416 40
Total expenditures for frontier and foreign missions for four years ending, April 30, 1861 ....$	45,238 44

HOME WORK.

Whole amount paid for home missionary labor for the four years ending April 30, 1861............$	81,829 91
Total for home, frontier, and foreign work...........$	127,063 35

INCIDENTAL EXPENSES OF THE BOARD.

Salaries.........$	1,176 28
Traveling expenses	738 28
Printing and mailing reports, certificates, missionary Telescope, &c., &c	2,443 97
Interest	1,291 87
Total..........$	5,650 40

CHAPTER IV.

Fourteenth General Conference — Wisconsin again made a Mission Conference — Cascade Conference Organized.

THE fourteenth General Conference of the United Brethren in Christ was held in Western College, Iowa, in May, 1865. At this date the Board had ten mission-conferences under its fostering care, namely:

Parkersburg, Missouri, Kansas, Oregon, California, Minnesota, Canada, Fox River, North Michigan, and Indiana German.

. The Indiana German Conference was, at this session of the General Conference, united with the Ohio German Conference, and consequently received no further assistance from the Board. The Wisconsin Conference, which is wanting in the above list, had been made self-supporting in 1861, when the Fox River Conference was organized out of a part of its territory. But at this General Conference it was again placed on the list of mission conferences, a decidedly unwise measure.

The Oregon Conference had become quite a strong body by this date. A goodly number of its members and ministers had emigrated to the Walla Walla valley, Washington Territory. So rapid had been the growth of the Church in this valley that the General Conference ordered that a new mission-conference be organized to be called Cascade—a name that was afterward exchanged for "WALLA WALLA." It also voted to make the Oregon a self-supporting conference.

One year after, Bishop Shuck reported to the corresponding secretary of the Missionary Society, the following figures for the Pacific Coast District:

Whole number of members...	1,209
Decrease in one year...	60
Itinerant preachers 20	
Local preachers..18—	38
Money collected for missions.......................................$ 191 00	
Money collected for preachers...................................	3,767 53

From the bishops' address at the same conference, I glean the following figures:

Whole number of members in the Church...............	89,911
Decrease in four years..	4,642
Increase in number of classes.............................	720
Number of meeting-houses.................................	207
Number of Sabbath-schools.................................	9,928
Number of Sabbath-school scholars.....................	68,171

The bishops state that they had no report from Kentucky, Tennessee, the Pacific Coast, or from that part of the Virginia and Parkersburg conferences within the rebel lines. Had these figures been obtained they would have shown that the Church had at least held its own during the war, instead of decreasing. as their figures show, 4,642.

The money expended for frontier and foreign works, and for conferences, is exhibited in the following table:

FOREIGN WORK.

Sherbro Mission—West Africa, for the quadrennial term ending April 30, 1865	$ 5,530 29

FRONTIER WORK.

Massachusetts Mission	793 68
Kentucky Missions	100 25
California Conference	1,351 00
Oregon Conference	900 00
Kansas Conference	1,415 83
Missouri Conference	1,308 80
Minnesota Conference	1,080 42
Tennessee Mission	206 00
Fox River Conference	850 00
North Michigan Conference	831 66
Canada Conference	1,185 28
Parkersburg Conference	805 15
Indiana German Conference	1,566 66
Nebraska Mission	50 00
Freedmen's Mission	10,170 81
Total sum paid by board to missionaries	$ 28,145 83
Salary paid missionaries by their fields	22,459 68
Total sum paid missionaries in the foreign and frontier fields	$ 50,605 51
The branch societies, or annual conferences, paid to home missionaries in the four years, including salary received on their fields	102,631 55
Total sum spent for foreign, frontier, and home work	$153,237 06

INCIDENTAL EXPENSES FOR THE FOUR YEARS ENDING APRIL 30, 1862.

On salaries and clerk-hire	$2,532 00
Interest and discount	972 30
Postage, stationery, expressage, and sundries	222 47
Printing annual reports and certificates	672 96
Plate for certificates	130 00
Traveling expenses	824 31
Total	$5,354 04

CHAPTER V.

Twelve Mission Conferences — North-Michigan Self-supporting — German Missions in Toledo and Columbus.

THE fifteenth General Conference was held in Lebanon, Pennsylvania, in the month of May, 1869. There were now thirty-eight annual conferences. Of these, thirty-three were represented in the General Conference, namely: Alleghany, Auglaize, Canada, East Des Moines, West Des Moines, Erie, Indiana, Illinois, Illinois Central, Iowa, North Iowa, Kansas, Miami, Muskingum, Michigan, North Michigan, Minnesota, Missouri, Ohio German, Pennsylvania, East Pennsylvania, Parkersburg, Rock River, Sandusky, St. Joseph, Scioto, Tennessee, Virginia, White River, Upper Wabash, Lower Wabash, Western Reserve, Wisconsin—33.

Not represented.—Cascade, Oregon, California, Kentucky, Fox River—5.

Of these thirty-eight conferences, twelve were on the list of mission-conferences, namely: Cascade, California, Kansas, Missouri, Minnesota, Wisconsin, Fox River, North

Michigan, Canada, Kentucky, Tennessee, and Parkersburg. The General Conference added to the list the Osage Conference, which was organized by Bishop Dickson in April, 1870, with twenty-one preachers. It includes in its territory a portion of southern Missouri, and southern Kansas. But the North Michigan Conference was made self-supporting, and denominated the Michigan Conference, and the hitherto Michigan Conference was now named "the North Ohio Conference." Thus the Board commenced the quadrennial term with twelve mission-conferences. In these conferences, and independent or detached missions, it employed eighty-seven missionaries, and three in the foreign work. There were also employed by the conferences on home fields, one hundred and ninety-three missionaries; making an aggregate of two hundred and eighty-three missionaries employed by the Church. These missionaries received an average salary of $294.63. This included all that was paid them by the Missionary Society, and the fields which they served. It can not be claimed that our missionaries work only for money. There is, perhaps, no equal number of men in the world who do so much work for so little pay.

The Bishops' Address at this General Conference showed that there were 89,811 members connected with the Church. This was a gain of 18,311 in four years—a very gratifying showing.

They also reported as follows:

Meeting-houses	1,400
Increase	152
Number of Sabbath-schools	2,268
Sabbath-school scholars	106,002
Money collected for Sabbath-school purposes	$100,000 00

During the quadrennial term the Board had aided the Ohio German Conference in establishing a mission among the Germans in Columbus, and another in Toledo, Ohio. It had also sent several missionaries to the southern part of the State of Illinois. These explanations will enable the reader to understand the following table, which shows what sums, and where the missionary money was expended.

FOREIGN FIELD.

Sherbro Mission—West Africa, for the quadrennial term ending April 30, 1869	$6,183 45

FRONTIER FIELD.

Canada Conference, for the quadrennial term ending April 30, 1869	1,355 54
Fox River Conference	1,300 00
Wisconsin Conference	1,096 53

HOME MISSIONS.

Cascade Conference	1,500 23
California Conference	1,560 82
Parkersburg Conference	1,800 00
Missouri Conference	3,479 15
Kansas Conference	1,638 27
Minnesota Conference	1,591 34
North Michigan Conference	1,321 00
Kentucky Conference	3,281 05
Tennessee Conference	3,601 34
Indiana German Conference	250 00
Columbus, Ohio, German Mission	700 00
Toledo, Ohio, German Mission	510 10
Southern Illinois Mission	1,842 75
Freedmen's Mission, Vicksburg, Mississippi	1,390 12
Dakota Mission	125 00
Southern Missouri Mission	142 00
Total sums paid to frontier and foreign missions in four years	$34,668 86
Salary paid missionaries by their fields for the quadrennial term ending April 30, 1869	$52,815 58
Whole amount paid frontier and foreign missionaries	$87,484 27

HOME MISSIONS.

Missionary money paid by branch treasurers, for the quadrennial term ending April 30, 1869	$69,701 13
Salaries paid to home missionaries for the quadrennial term ending April 30, 1869	118,538 40
Whole amount paid to home, frontier, and foreign missionaries	$275,723 80

MISCELLANEOUS EXPENDITURES FOR THE FOUR YEARS ENDING APRIL 30, 1869.

Salaries	$3,768 75
Traveling expenses of Board and officers	938 99
Expressage, postage, and stationery	238 56
Interest, discount, and exchange	134 01
Printing annual reports, certificates, etc	1,395 16
Mission-room rent, and other expenses	208 87
	$6,684 24

SYNOPSIS OF THE WHOLE WORK, MAY, 1869.

HOME MISSIONS.

Number of mission fields	177
Number of appointments	763
Number of meeting-houses	154
Number of church-members	15,250
Number of Sabbath-schools	350
Number of teachers	2,332
Number of scholars	15,179

FRONTIER AND FOREIGN FIELDS.

Number of mission fields	96
Number of appointments	638
Number of meeting-houses	44
Number of church-members	7,649
Number of Sabbath-schools	240
Number of teachers	1,094
Number of scholars	7,585

EXPENDITURES IN SIXTEEN YEARS.

For the quadrennial term ending April 30, 1857	$ 81,681 21
For the quadrennial term ending April 30, 1861	127,063 35
For the quadrennial term ending April 30, 1865	152,898 66
For the quadrennial term ending April 30, 1869	275,723 80
Total	$637,367 02

CHAPTER VI.

Increase in Numbers—Improvement in Book-keeping—Financial Exhibit of Twenty Years—Sixteenth General Conference, in Dayton, Ohio.

IF the reader has scrutinized the foregoing tables, he has been impressed with two conclusions of great importance. The first is that the United Brethren Church has steadily increased ever since the organization of the Missionary Society, if not at a rapid, yet creditable and reliable rate. In some localities the progress has been quite slow; in others there has been an actual decline; but in the aggregate the increase has been much more noticeable and permanent than it was prior to 1853. The second conclusion is, that while the Church has increased rapidly in numbers, wealth, and benevolent contributions, she has also advanced in the art of book-keeping, and collecting, systematizing, preserving, and publishing statistics. Of course, the reader must not think that all the increase and improvement the Church has made in the last two decades is wholly owing to the efforts of the Missionary Society. The colleges have exerted a vast influence, both in adding to the sum total of the intelligence of the Church, and the spirit of beneficence, that have surpassed the highest expectations of the most sanguine. But making due allowance for the influence of the colleges, the printing establishment, and other agencies not necessary here to mention, it still remains true that the Missionary Society has, under the blessing of God, wrought an untold and incalculable amount of good, both in the work of evangelization itself, and in cultivating the graces of a Christian character on the part of the membership at large.

The sixteenth General Conference, which met in May, 1873, in Dayton, Ohio, was the largest ecclesiastical body ever assembled in the denomination. There were forty-two organized annual conferences in the connection at this date. Of this number, *thirty-eight* were represented by delegates on the floor of the General Conference, namely: Alleghany, Auglaize, Canada, Central Illinois, Colorado, East Des Moines, East German, East Pennsylvania, Erie, Fox River, Illinois, Indiana, Iowa, Kansas, Lower Wabash, Miami, Michigan, Minnesota, Missouri, Muskingum, North

Iowa, North Ohio, Ohio German, Oregon, Osage, Parkersburg, Pennsylvania, Rock River, Sandusky, Scioto, Southern Illinois, St. Joseph, Upper Wabash, Virginia, West Des Moines, Western Reserve, White River, Wisconsin—38.

Not represented.—California, Cascade, Dacota, Tennessee—4.

It is proper to remark that delegates were elected for these four unrepresented conferences, but they failed to attend; also, that Oregon, Colorado, Osage, and Southern Illinois, had but one delegate each, in attendance; West Des Moines, and Minnesota had two delegates in the conference, making the total number of delegates composing the Conference one hundred and four. Add to this the four bishops, who also have a vote in the General Conference, and it will be seen there were present one hundred and eight members.

Of the forty-two, fourteen were mission-conferences, to wit: Cascade,—whose name was very properly changed by this General Conference to Walla Walla,—California, Colorado, Osage, Kansas, Missouri, Dakota, Minnesota, Fox River, Wisconsin, Southern Illinois, Tennessee, Parkersburg, and Canada. Oregon Conference, which had been self-supporting for eight years, was again reduced to a mission-conference. A mission-conference was also ordered for the State of Nebraska, making in all, sixteen mission-conferences. But the General Conference also voted that after the second session succeeding the present session of the General Conference, the Parkersburg, Kansas, Missouri, and Wisconsin conferences should become self-supporting, thus leaving the Missionary Society with the care of one dozen mission-conferences.

THE BISHOPS' ADDRESS.

This document, always important, was of unusual interest at this session, as, in a few words it recounted, in actual statistics, substantial progress in all the elements that go to make up an active and strong church, capable of accomplishing much in the advancement of the Master's kingdom.

Number of church-members	125,658
Increase in four years	17,347
Number of meeting-houses	1,657
Increase in four years	257
Number of Sunday-schools	2,662
Number of scholars	128,425
Increase in the number of schools	756
Increase in the number of scholars	22,423

They add that in addition to supporting themselves the Sabbath-schools had during the term contributed $4,000 for the General Sabbath-school Association, and that the collections for this purpose were steadily increasing from year to year.

The corresponding secretary's report showed that the Missionary Society now employed three hundred and thirteen laborers, and that their average salary was $296. Eight of these missionaries were in foreign fields, one hundred and twenty-three in frontier fields, and one hundred and eighty-two in home fields.

Amount of missionary money contributed by the Church	$ 49,227 35
Salaries paid by fields served by missionaries	52,420 39
Total	$101,647 74

EXPENDITURES IN FOUR YEARS.

Bavaria Mission, Germany	$ 2,216 18
Sherbro Mission, West Africa	13,985 45
Canada Conference	1,849 55
Fox River Conference	1,577 59
Wisconsin Conference	930 19
Minnesota Conference	1,660 88
Dacotah Conference	1,583 87
Cascade Conference	2,556 09
California Conference	2,113 09
Colorado Conference	2,616 03
Osage Conference	2,068 68
Kansas Conference	1,286 95

HOME MISSIONS.

Missouri Conference	1,069 10
Southern Illinois Conference	3,190 32
Tennessee Conference	3,079 92
Parkersburg Conference	2,315 00
Kentucky missions	1,096 54
Columbus, Ohio, German Mission	2,569 02
Toledo, Ohio, German Mission	1,826 37
Southwestern Missouri Mission, for 1870	57 00
Freedmen's Mission, Virginia	188 05
Harrisburg, Pennsylvania, German Mission	100 25
Nebraska Mission	100 00
Philadelphia German Mission	10 00
Total	$ 49,700 48
Salaries in mission conferences, including the sums paid by branch treasurers	$ 58,813 77
Total paid to frontier and foreign missions	$108,514 25

HOME MISSIONS.

Paid to missionaries by branch treasurers	$ 86,979 81
Paid missionaries by fields, as salary	165,276 41
Total to home missions	$252,256 22
Total to home, frontier, and foreign work	$360,770 47

MISCELLANEOUS EXPENDITURES FOR FOUR YEARS.

On salaries	$ 7,025 58
Traveling expenses	1,926 25
Stationery, expressage, postage, telegrams	366 79
Interest, exchange, taxes, revenue stamps	364 81
Printing annual reports, circulars, etc	1,460 23
Fuel, light, repairs	148 65
For Kansas tent	395 40
Lawyer's and court charges	44 15
To secretaries of annual meetings	13 00
For the education and support of D. F. Wilberforce	213 69
To J. P. Morris, guardian of Rev. I. Sloan's children	200 00
Money lost by the mails	8 00
For pencil-sketch for new certificate	90 00
Blank books for records	8 60
Total miscellaneous expenditures	$12,265 15

HOME MISSIONS.

FINANCIAL EXHIBIT OF TWENTY YEARS.

The Missionary Society expended during the first
quadrennial term, ending April, 30, 1857......$ 81,681 21
For the second term, ending April 30, 1861.......... 127,063 35
For the third term, ending April 30, 1865........... 152,898 66
For the fourth term, ending April 30, 1869.......... 275,723 80
For the fifth term, ending April 30, 1873........... 360,770 47

Total...$998,137 49

www.ingramcontent.com/pod-product-compliance
Lightning Source LLC
Chambersburg PA
CBHW032109230426
43672CB00009B/1689